Shelby's Grace

From Abused Pup to Angel of Mercy

Joe Dwyer

SHELBY
Perennial Press Publishing

For more information contact:
shelby@shelbysgrace.com

Book design by:
www.arborbooks.com

Printed in the United States of America

Shelby's Grace: From Abused Pup to Angel of Mercy
Joe Dwyer

1. Title   2. Author   3. Pets/Inspirational/Motivational

Library of Congress Control Number: 2010932121

ISBN 13: 978-0-6153862-8-7

To Shelby for being part of my life, for renewing my life, for empowering my purpose and for teaching me the meaning of forgiveness while inspiring me to go forth with you on your mission to serve and administer to people in need;

To all who love, respect and are willing to rescue and adopt abused and abandoned animals from shelters, welcoming them in your lives, homes and hearts as family members;

To those who love and accept pit bulls as gentle, nurturing pets— those who understand that unconditional love means saying no to the injurious and prejudicial breed/racial profiling of all God's creatures;

And to the memory of my beloved Fritz, best friend and 'brother' during my childhood and teens...

...this book is lovingly dedicated.

TABLE OF CONTENTS

ACKNOWLEDGMENTS

I wish to pay tribute to the very special individuals who share my love, passion and mission to rescue and open their hearts and homes to abused, neglected and abandoned dogs, regardless of their breed. You continue to give me peace as well as the encouragement and hope that prejudicial breed stereotyping with its detrimental consequences to innocent pups will be defeated.

To Nancy Thompson, I extend heartfelt thanks. It would have been an impossible quest for me to even have material to write this book without her support and intervention in rescuing Shelby.

I am also grateful to the Bloomfield Animal Shelter for offering refuge to Shelby and for seeing in her a reason to preserve her life. Thanks also to the volunteers and philanthropists who generously contribute time and funds to allow shelters across the nation to house and care for neglected dogs.

I am eternally grateful to Dr. Christopher Hunt, Shelby's surgeon, and the exceptional staff at the Animal Emergency and

Referral Associates for their incredible part in repairing her legs and making her dream of becoming a therapy dog a reality.

A very big thank you to Bright and Beautiful Therapy Dogs for confirming my opinion of Shelby's awesome talent and vocation to give back and serve humanity as a therapy dog.

My gratitude goes to Sue Falduto for her wonderful photo shoot. With her creativity and patience, she captured the true essence of Shelby.

A very heartfelt thanks to Nancy Genovese for her guidance in writing this book. Her love and dedication to both me and Shelby will never be forgotten.

To my wonderful family, Mom, Dad, Geralynn, Joe III and Jenna, and my extended canine family, Rommel, Greta and Spartacus, I express deep gratitude for their abundant love, support and patience in accepting Shelby into their lives.

I wish to give special mention to Shelby, my beloved pit bull, who has filled my life with joy, teaching me the meaning of unconditional love, loyalty, devotion, forgiveness and passion to assist all those who suffer. Thank you, Shelby—you are a beautiful gift from God.

"Life for life, eye for eye, tooth for tooth"—I rescued your life, Shelby—you rescued mine.

This book is born to honor all who believe in the sanctity of life, be it human or animal.

The Die Is Cast

*"If I have any beliefs about immortality, it is certain dogs I
have known will go to heaven, and very very few persons."*
—James Thurber

Something was not quite right. Why did I always feel lethargic—why were my after-school hours and weekends filled with monotony? Why wasn't I outgoing and vibrant, like most eleven-year-olds?

Childhood was usually a time of exploration, excitement and just having fun. So why was I always hindered by a heavy heart? I was healthy and growing, but why was I energy-deficient? Often it seemed as if the gel of a non-existent humidity had invaded my body and dampened my spirit, removing all the spunk and enthusiasm typical of boyhood.

Young and inexperienced, I lacked the knowledge to define, let alone remedy, the situation. Although I knew something was missing, it was far greater than my child's mind could fathom. Consequently, as most children believe, I continued to hope I would awaken one morning and everything would be different.

But what was wrong? Why did I sit for hours, brooding with my gaze fixed firmly on my dangling feet, swinging like the pendulum of a clock? I had loving, nurturing parents and a trauma-free childhood characterized neither by excruciating hardship nor undue distress, except for the standard growing pains every individual experiences en route to adulthood.

The unanswered questions led me to solicit God's help. Shortly thereafter, though totally uninformed of the mysterious workings of the Lord's intricate strategies, my prayer was answered.

Years later while undertaking studies for ordination as a deacon in the Roman Catholic Church, one of the required courses I pursued was centered on the Holy Scriptures. Excited and energized to be able to reread and reinterpret the Bible from a very different, 'professional' perspective, I began to understand more deeply how God's intentions and design for the Universe and its inhabitants were pertinent in modern times. But more importantly, I noticed how relevant His lessons were for me.

I also recognized the sheer mastery and validity of God's desire for all His creatures, man and animal, to co-exist in harmony, sharing reciprocal love and respect. According to the biblical expression of God's intention, the world did not belong exclusively to human beings. There were four-legged creatures and winged beings, sentient creatures like mankind, born with equal needs for nourishment, respect and the right to be treated with kindness and dignity.

All infused with the Lord's breath, they played a specific role in the Divine Plan—a purpose for being summoned to earth. In due time, I became aware of the influence this special design exercised in my own life.

Eventually I discovered that the mysterious lethargy, apathy and coldness within resulted from a cavernous, dark crater built of loneliness. It was deep. It was hollow. It was an enormous vacancy, impossible to fill. I was an only child, a lonesome boy.

After school and on weekends, when my parents were occupied, I sat closed in my own thoughts, longing for a companion with whom I could discuss the joys, sorrows, fears and uncertainties of life. The older I grew, the more pronounced became the yearning and the more manifest my failure to find someone to accompany me on my road to manhood.

"Joe, it's such a nice day. Why don't you go outside and play instead of just sitting moping in your room?" my mom would say, as she scurried about completing her Saturday morning tasks. "Later you can accompany your dad into town and help him with his errands."

Though I was fortunate to have adoring, doting parents, both of whom I loved dearly, neither suggestion was a thrilling option to an eleven-year-old boy, with a voracious appetite for a best friend.

"Okay, Mom," I shouted, making my way into the yard, obedient at least on this particular occasion. But my dilemma was far from resolved. Who would I play with? Who would I talk to and laugh with? What fun could I have all by myself?

"Why wasn't I blessed with a brother or sister like most of the children in my class?" I murmured, kicking the twigs that had fallen after the evening's windstorm.

Suffering from terrible, annoying skin allergies, I was not even permitted to have a pet for company. Whenever I asked, "Why can't we have a dog?" my parents would respond, "Joe, the dermatologist discouraged us from bringing a dog into the house. He believes the animal's fur would aggravate your skin allergies. When you get better, you may certainly have a dog."

I had something to hope for. Did I see a tiny flicker of light amid the gloomy shadows of my loneliness? One thing was sure—I was not going to dwell on my skin issues as a life-ruining dilemma.

A positive attitude in conjunction with understanding, caring parents who took me to endless specialists strengthened my determination, teaching me the merits of tenacity. During one visit after I had been scrutinized under a scorching bright light and magnifying lens to get a clear view of my lesions, the physician cleared his throat.

Realizing this habit usually preceded a vocal message, I shut my eyes and wished for the words I so desperately longed to hear.

"Mr. Dwyer," the physician began. I held my breath. "Joe's skin allergies have subsided. He has made great progress and I do believe he is well on the way to recovery. Therefore, I see absolutely no reason why he cannot have a short-haired little dog."

A dog—I could have a dog! My heart thumped several multiple-bounce drum rolls, building anticipation of an oncoming joy. My stomach somersaulted in unison with the beats. Excitedly I searched for my dad's eyes. Would he keep his promise?

The glow of his happy gaze told me I would soon have a pet. Quickly I turned toward Mom. This was too important; I needed verification. Her radiant smile confirmed she was in total agreement with Dad. Elated, I did not drift off to sleep that evening. Instead I daydreamed about the soon-to-arrive new pet.

Several days later, Mom, Dad and I embarked on a mission to find a little short-haired dog. "How will we know which dog to pick?" I said, shouting above the din of barks and whines. Grinning, my dad lowered a tiny dog to the floor. "This is Fritz," he announced. "He will be coming home with us."

With his stunted, bent legs, barrel chest and the longest torso I had ever seen on a dog, Fritz immediately won my heart.

"Maybe I have someone to play with," I whispered under my breath. Excited to have my very own playmate, I leaned over to pet his head. Uncertain of my intentions and newfound exuberance, the puppy turned his head.

"He doesn't like me," I said, taking a step back.

"Give him a little time to get to know you," Dad blurted. "I'm sure you'll become great friends." What foresight! Though I was unaware at the time, I later discovered that my dad's words were the gospel truth.

That evening, with Fritz in my room, I started the first of endless dialogues I would have with him throughout the years. Cradling his little head in my hands, I lowered my face to his. "Fritz," I whispered, "you are my brother!"

Thus began my loving liaison with a four-pawed creature, a relationship that would set the stage for my extraordinary camaraderie with Shelby decades later. A very exceptional affiliation, this relationship with the sweet, mistreated pit bull would alter my life and the lives of others, forever.

A reddish-tan Dachshund with teasing, playful eyes, Fritz had an emotional personality, manifested by the numerous ways in which he wagged his tail when in my company. Eventually I learned how to determine his state of mind and heart by observing the position, movement and shape of his tail.

Between brothers, there should be reciprocity. This is the glue that bonds the relationship—any relationship. Therefore, if I wanted Fritz to understand and love me, I had to love and understand him. Unlike humans, who have a multitude of possessions, animals have just one—their life. Hence it was up to me to make sure his one prized possession would give him happiness.

Within a few short days, I realized I had the best friend I always coveted—the 'brother' I dreamed about and prayed for. Of course, never in my wildest reveries would I have imagined my bosom buddy with four paws and a tail! But one of the most enthralling features of life is the unpredictable nature of situations and circumstances. Actually not knowing what or who lies around the corner makes the journey more riveting.

Then again, when the Lord created living beings, He intended all His creatures to share the world in harmony.

Our relationship grew. Upon my return from school and the completion of my homework, chores and extracurricular activities, Fritz and I met for a daily rendezvous. Astute and vigilant, as soon as he spotted me changing my clothes, he would jump on the bed, eager to be my sounding board and offer a shoulder to cry on. Dancing eyes and a set of erect ears signaled that Doxie, as I playfully called him at times, was ready to hear the day's events and whatever else occupied my mind.

Throughout the years Fritz learned of my joys and sorrows, my fears over mid-term and final exams, my insecurities with girls and the mounting peer pressure in school. Attentively he listened to my questions, anxieties and frustrations. There was nothing Fritz and I couldn't discuss—there were no boundaries, no censorship, no qualms he would ever betray a trust.

In the role of contrite confessor, Fritz heard my admissions of mistakes and the endless slips and falls I experienced, gentling licking my tears when I cried or stretching his neck to rest his little head on my knees to offer comfort when I was upset.

Ignorant of greed and egotistical demands, Doxie neither interrupted a conversation to go outside nor wavered his concentration even when I complained about my parents, whom he loved dearly. But as all growing children, I soon yearned for independence, seeking more liberty and less adult guidance in my life, though Mom and Dad, not necessarily in agreement with the timing, were reticent to grant.

Best of all, despite his bouts of epilepsy, Fritz was always there for me, treating me with love and respect, teaching me how to love unconditionally and greet the new day with optimism. He taught me how to enjoy and appreciate the blessings of nature, like feeling the wind tousle my hair and the cooling breeze dry the beads of sweat forming along my forehead as I ran outdoors while he tried to keep pace, panting and bouncing on his undersized legs.

Like a radiant, variegated rainbow splashed across the sky after a summer storm, my sullen frown turned into a full-tooth smile. Laughter and chatter substituted a silent sulking. Lethargy gave way to exuberance. No longer a mere spectator in life, I became an enthusiastic participant.

With his loving, feisty, extroverted nature, Fritz pulled me out from the cocoon into which I had crawled. No longer timid, insecure and withdrawn, I confronted my growing years with a more aggressive, spirited attitude. In return I gave my little 'brother' unconditional love, trust and loyalty.

Our relationship deepened throughout the months and years, as I shared my innermost thoughts with my 'brother' and confidante, discussing all the major events, issues and crises of my young life. Fritz offered solidarity during my initial dating years when I had little, if any, knowledge of the female species. Girls were a mystery, fun to be with, but complicated and frustrating. Yet when I discussed my women-oriented dilemmas with Fritz, I was able to work through the darkness even though I did not always see the light.

Though Fritz suffered from epilepsy, God granted him a long life. In fact, he lived long enough to play a major role when, as a young man, I fell in love with Geralynn and planned to ask for her hand in marriage.

"Fritz, I will bring Geralynn here so you can meet her," I told him after confessing she had won my heart. "I'm certain you will love her as I do."

By now Fritz's opinion and approval were of vital importance. We had gone through middle school, high school, and college, as well as my initiation in the work force, together, and everything in between; therefore, there was absolutely no way I would even minimally consider isolating him from this momentous step in my life. To do so would be an unpardonable insult.

Somewhat anxious, I organized the meeting. The evening preceding the encounter, I informed Fritz of my intention to ask Geralynn to marry me—"But only if you approve," I reassured.

Anxious and nervous, I realized the situation I had put myself in. What if Fritz did not feel my fiancée was the right girl? Restless, I twisted and turned, beating my pillow as if it were the cause of my insomnia. Fritz, on the other hand, snored like a 250-pound wrestler. He didn't seem the least bit concerned. Perhaps after all these years, he trusted my judgment. I prayed for added security. "Lord, please let Fritz and Geralynn hit it off."

The following evening, I gave Fritz a bath and brushed his shiny fur. Not only was I concerned about his opinion of Geralynn, but I was also worried about her feelings toward Fritz. It had to be perfect—it was far too risky.

Geralynn arrived, eager to meet the by-now-infamous Fritz—my 'brother,' best friend and confidante. Would they bond? Would Fritz coil and withdraw or would he warm to her?

After sniffing around Geralynn's feet for a few seconds, Fritz hesitantly raised his penetrating glance, locking eyes with her. I waited, not daring to breathe, holding my gaze on Fritz's lowered tail. It was motionless. My heart raced. Why wasn't he wagging his tail?

Geralynn and I exchanged glances. From the corner of my eye I noticed Fritz's tail flutter. Seconds later it began wagging in a slow, steady sweep. I bent down to pet his head: Geralynn imitated my affectionate gesture. Fritz raised his tail, wagging it at super speed. His tiny paws quivered then danced in excitement just before he nuzzled her hand. Gathering him in her arms, she joyfully accepted his multitude of wet, sticky licks on her cheeks. My prayer was answered. Fritz was in love with Geralynn.

So as not to disturb his familiar lifestyle when I married, Fritz remained with my parents. I visited him almost daily until his death at sixteen years of age, two years succeeding the birth of my first-born. His passing was peaceful, painless and quick—my sadness and grief intense, excruciating and long-lasting. He is still mourned, twenty years thereafter.

Then it happened—Shelby entered my life. An engaging, beautiful pit bull with a melancholy glance that spoke of hidden agonies, she had no idea of the journey we would take together. Neither did I. However, her untold secrets of physical and psychological abuse did little to conceal a nurturing heart and a saintly ability to forgive. Still, I had not the slightest inkling regarding the extraordinary impact her phenomenal presence would exercise on all who would enjoy her presence in their lives.

Our meeting was a reciprocal life-saving blessing of Divine Intervention. Like Julius Caesar, I had crossed the Rubicon. There was no turning back. The die was cast!

Rendezvous
with Destiny

"Dogs are our link to paradise. They don't know evil or jealousy or discontent. To sit with a dog on a hillside on a glorious afternoon is to be back in Eden, where doing nothing was not boring—it was peace."
——Milan Kundera

There exists a natural remedy available to all. It is a potent tonic with the power to liberate living beings from the doldrums of misery. It is also an analgesic, numbing the stinging pain radiating from some of life's more agonizing torments. That remedy is a panacea called love. Though exceedingly precious, it costs absolutely nothing in dollars and cents.

Beyond definition, beyond measure and way past the intangible, love's magical benefits are coveted across the Seven Seas—and not exclusively by men, women and children.

Few, perhaps, understand better than I how the amazing influence of love extends further than mankind—not because there is a lack of knowledge, but possibly because there is a lack of personal experience. The truth is, unlike math or science, love can be neither taught nor learned. Instead, to have life, love must be lived—love must be experienced in all its many nuances.

During the early hours of an otherwise ordinary but blustery

January afternoon, I headed over to the Bloomfield Animal Shelter, in Bloomfield, New Jersey, to visit some of my four-pawed friends and perhaps greet some new arrivals.

I was a volunteer for the past year and a half, and my heart went out to the many abandoned animals, longing for a loving pat on the head, or just a few sporadic moments of undivided attention all living beings crave. Alone and neglected, they were lonely for the human companionship they either forfeited through no fault of their own, or never had the pleasure to experience.

Several weeks earlier, around Thanksgiving, I had been introduced to Harrison, a stunning husky whose thick, soft, silvery gray coat I envied in the gelid first weeks of the New Jersey winter.

Harrison, I was told, suffered from severe debilitating arthritis in his pelvic region, an incapacitating condition that quashed any hope of either his owner returning or his suitability for adoption. Consequently, Harrison's fate was sealed.

The wag of his tail upon my arrival was too authentic not to believe; therefore, I had the confirmation my presence brought him some measure of happiness. Of course the feeling was mutual, and in a short time he was part of my life. Harrison and I were buddies.

Our visits became extended as our friendship deepened until sad tidings were delivered.

"Joe," the shelter coordinator said one afternoon, "I'm afraid I have some devastating news."

My heart grew heavy as I came to terms with the inevitable. It was stronger than a suspicion that Harrison's health worsened. His pain was excruciating; he could no longer rise up on his legs. Furthermore his appetite had waned, depriving him of vital nutrients.

"Joe, I know you are very attached to Harrison," the coordinator continued, "but it would be cruel and inhumane to prolong his agony. His condition is degenerative and quickly progressing. I'm afraid we will have to euthanize him to end his misery. I'm certain you understand and agree."

Like daggers hurled from across the room, his anticipated, though much-dreaded, words pierced my skin. While reason reassured me the vet's decision was justified, emotionally I was crushed. Since Harrison's quality of life was pitiful, it was only right to dismiss him from his torment. There was no other solution. I had to accept the fact that he had traveled as far as he could. The end comes for all—man and animal—and we must be resigned to the law of God.

Three days before Christmas, I said a tearful goodbye to Harrison, rubbed his back for the last time and watched sadly as his life force waned. Minutes later his breathing became shallow, his round, sparkling eyes disappeared behind heavy lids, his arthritis-ridden body stiffened and his heart ceased beating. Looking at his shut eyes, my own filled with tears.

Watching him go, I reflected in silence. Despite the atrocious suffering, Harrison had experienced human love and compassion, maybe for the first time. Unaware of his life story, or the reasons for his crippling malady, I was certain he was in peace. That in itself offered me a morsel of solace in my sadness. Then I went home and mourned the loss of a dear friend.

With the arrival of the holidays and some rather pressing business and family events to consolidate, I put my shelter visits on hold. Shortly thereafter, around the end of January, a longing for my abandoned friends came racing back with added intensity, drawing me back to the shelter.

"Hi, Joe, happy new year," one of the volunteers shouted, spotting my entry. "We missed seeing you around here. Where have you been?"

"Family and holidays—you know how it is," I blurted. "But I'm back to see my friends."

"Well, we have some newcomers I think you might enjoy meeting."

"Okay, I'm ready—make the introductions!" I responded, always excited at the possibility to make the acquaintance of new dogs.

"There is one dog in particular I think you'll love to meet. She's a real beauty. Shelby is her name."

"Take me to her," I rebutted, eager to make a new friend, especially since I was still mourning the loss of Harrison. He had surely left a vacancy in my heart—one that needed to be filled. However, as in human friendships, not every relationship is the same. There are varying degrees of feelings—inexplicable and uncontrollable; perhaps it's the chemistry theory.

The volunteer accompanied me to a large pen in an area somewhat shielded from the elements. Sometimes when it snowed in New Jersey, it would be reported in feet, not inches. But regardless of the inclement weather, the animals were always made as comfortable as possible. The Bloomfield, New Jersey, shelter was dedicated to respecting the exigencies of all its 'guests.'

"Shelby is over there," the volunteer said, pointing his index finger toward one of the last cages. "That's her. Why don't you introduce yourself and take her for a walk? Maybe she'll go with you. "

I needed no further encouragement. Stepping over some still-uncrushed twigs and a tangle of brown blades of grass that had been burnt from the cold and weight of several early season snowstorms, I darted over to Shelby.

"Hello, Shelby," I said softly, not to scare her. "I'm Joe. I hear you are the new girl here."

Peering warily from an adorable though wasted face, a pair of expressive pale green eyes lifted to meet mine. The impact was overwhelming. *"There is something very special about Shelby,"* I whispered, feeling a magnetic draw to her.

She was breathtakingly beautiful, but a striking sadness hinted, careful not to give away the details of a probably aching secret buried within. Shelby sat quivering, huddled in the back of a twenty-by-six-foot pen—a shuddering from within. My intuition told me it had no link to a cool body temperature.

The sun shone on her tan/white brindle coat, enhancing the

pure cloud of white fur delicately designed to form a triangle running from the top of her head to under her chin, dismissing any attribution of blame on nature. Although Shelby was shivering, she did not feel cold. She was cold—cold inside, a bitter, existential cold.

Frail and apparently malnourished, the new 'guest' at Bloomfield, an interesting pit bull mix, resembled a skeleton used to teach freshman veterinary students canine anatomy! My first impression was despondent. Unlike most dogs, Shelby seemed unresponsive to my attentions. No tail wag, no excitement in her eyes.

"Hello, Shelby," I insisted, trying to get a reaction, one way or another. "Come here, I'd like to get to know you." Shelby lowered her gaze. Still, in spite of her reluctance, I was convinced she was special. Refusing to relinquish my courtship even after multiple rejections, I felt certain I would eventually break the ice.

Leaning over, I slowly extended my hand toward her head, making certain it was in full view of her eyes. My instinct moved me to establish a physical contact. She was so beautiful, how could I not touch her? However, Shelby's body language led me to withdraw for fear of scaring her. First impressions are important and I did not want her to form a less than positive opinion about me. After all, I already had designs on her.

"Hello, Shelby," I greeted her softly. "It's so nice to see you. How are you today?"

Shelby eyed me stoically but did not rise from her reclining position. Inching closer, I hoped she would perhaps meet me halfway. No luck. *Was my charm fading?* I questioned. Usually I had an easy time with dogs. They seemed to respond to my gestures of friendship, always thrilled to receive my love and intentions. Apparently Shelby was different. Perhaps she had endured some trauma at the hands of a human. I had to be patient, but I was determined.

I edged closer. But Shelby did not budge.

"Hey, Shelby," I continued with a stronger voice, believing I could snap her out of the lethargy. She tried to stand but slumped over several times before succeeding. Once she was on all fours, I noticed a series of pronounced scars on her hind legs. Wide, round, circular areas, red and hairless, decorated both thighs. I wanted to caress them. I longed to gently rub my fingers in the raw, bald spots, hoping I could alleviate any soreness.

"What happened to you, Shelby?" I questioned, not sure I wanted the answer. She was too young to be afflicted with arthritis and those big disfiguring scars spoke of a horror I wanted to deny.

"Joe," the volunteer said, sensing sparkling chemistry between us, "I see you're getting acquainted with Shelby. Isn't she a beauty? Why don't you take her for a walk?"

I didn't need a second invitation, though I wondered how she would react to my act of human kindness. Would she recoil in fear? Would she react to my advances with aggression or rejection? Regardless, I was not shying away.

"Shelby," I called, "please come over here." Amazingly, she obeyed, taking a few unsteady steps. I held my breath, thanking God for her reaction. As she neared, dragging her body, I could see the pain in her young face. It was heartbreaking.

Pulling open the gate to her pen, I gently slid the leash around her neck. My hand brushed against the soft fur on the back of her neck for the first time. Instantly we connected. I knew right then there was a great deal more to this meeting. Furthermore, my initial hunch was confirmed—Shelby was a very special dog. Of course, it was too soon to know why.

Unwilling to cause her any discomfort, I held the leash loosely and gently coaxed her to walk. She obliged for about thirty or forty yards, right to the entrance of the shelter before stopping short and plopping down with a muffled thud, like a bag of potatoes suddenly dropped to the floor.

"What's up, Shelby? It's a nice day—don't you want to walk a little farther? Are you in a lot of pain?"

Shelby in the shelter.

The look in her eyes told me she had had enough. Not one to force an issue against someone's will, man or animal, I accompanied her back to the pen. Once inside, she turned her head in my direction and I noticed a very subtle movement of her tail. Though not quite a sweeping wag, it fluttered a couple of times. *Was she thanking me for my company?* I mused.

Quickly I went over to the treat counter to get something for Shelby to communicate my joy. However, when I raised it to her mouth, she turned her head in refusal. Gazing around the pen, I noted her bowl was full. Shelby was not accepting nourishment. That explained her extreme frailty.

I left the shelter invigorated, like a man who had just spotted a new love to pursue. Additionally, at the time, for my business I was enrolled in a professional dog-training program with course work requiring a set amount of hours at a shelter. How perfect was that!

Returning to the shelter to visit Shelby at least twice a week, I spoke to and walked many of my canine friends, though no one dared doubt my intentions were centered on the darling pit bull. She was different from the other 'guests' in the shelter, and I soon realized she had to be treated with kid gloves, like a fairy-tale princess. And I was ready to step into the role of a gallant knight in shining armor, coming to rescue a damsel in distress.

Her whimpering whenever she tried to stand, her unbalanced stride as she walked, her tendency to put pressure only on her front legs and her reluctance to trust narrated a terrifying story, the circumstances of which I was anxious to learn.

Did Shelby have a nasty accident? Was it a hit and run? Or was it something totally different?

Various scenarios unwound in my mind. Every time the scene changed, I squirmed. Whatever or whomever harmed Shelby pushed her into post-traumatic stress syndrome, but God sent me to her rescue. Our paths crossed for a reason. It was up to me to untie the knots in the thread of her life.

Despite my initial feeling of sympathy for Shelby, I had to admit there was a certain romantic twist to the aura of melancholy surrounding the pit bull puppy whose gaze had locked with mine.

What lies behind Shelby's sadness? I repeated over and over like a mantra, actually spending sleepless nights searching for answers. She was such a young dog, maybe in the final months of puppy-hood, judging from her still relatively disproportionate paws, yet her diffidence and unavailability to human kindness was that of an adult dog who had lived a lifetime of disillusionment and sadness.

However, fascinated, I knew I would pursue until I had answers. More importantly, I would pursue until I had won her love and trust. At that moment I had no idea what an exhilarating journey I was about to embark on.

The Courtship

"The love of our living creatures is the most noble attribute of man."

—Charles Darwin

Following my initial meeting with Shelby, I was unable to clear my mind of the ever-present vision of her sweet face encased in an aura of such penetrating melancholy. Lured by her unmistakable secret, I spent several restless nights orchestrating various scenarios in a desperate attempt to piece together a possible sequence of events that could have contributed to the pitiful state of this innocent, defenseless animal.

Sighing prior to hurling off the covers, I awoke shortly after sunrise; my solace rested in Shelby's rescue. Though it was a blessing, it was certainly not without trauma, the extent of which was unknown until later. However, her good fate was not sufficient. To quench my thirst for answers, I had to resolve the terrible mystery behind Shelby's glowering demeanor.

Returning to the Bloomfield shelter, I assumed a Sherlock Holmes persona, of course without the quirks of either stuffing the toe of a Persian slipper with tobacco or spearing my documents with a jack knife prior to filing them on the mantle. But with the relentlessly questioning mind of the legendary private eye, I began investigating.

"I'd like some information about Shelby," I said, addressing the coordinator upon entering the shelter. "If possible, I'd like to speak with the person who brought her here. Do you have a name?"

"Nancy Thompson is the person to speak to," he responded, pointing his finger in the direction of a blond woman of medium stature, dressed in a crisp navy uniform. "Nancy is responsible for Shelby's rescue."

"Thanks," I muttered. Turning in Nancy's direction, I did not need any further coaxing. Several seconds thereafter, I reached my destination.

"Hello, Nancy—I'm interested in learning some info about that pit bull," I said, gazing and pointing in Shelby's direction.

"Hi, Joe—it's always nice to see you here among these poor, abandoned dogs. They certainly appreciate a little love and attention, just like the rest of us." Her warm smile was a perfect fit with her altruistic personality.

Unbuttoning my jacket, I prepared myself for a lengthy chat with Nancy.

"Nancy, what's the scoop on Shelby?" I said, spinning on my heels to face her pen—the pit bull pup. "She seems to be in pain—as if she experienced some kind of distress. Was she hit by a car?"

"No, Joe, I'm afraid it's a bit more complicated."

I swallowed hard in anticipation of a story my intuition told me would be difficult to digest.

"One day I received a call from the Bloomfield police. The officer told me there was a dog fastened to a fence at the Shell station, right under the Garden State Parkway. It was their feeling the dog had been abandoned for at least two days.

"'Poor pup,'" the officer said. She was trembling from fright and from the atrocious pandemonium of the overhead traffic. When I arrived at the Shell station," Nancy continued, "I noticed the dog had been untied and sat beside the officer, near his car. One glance told me she had been badly abused prior to her abandonment."

What was Nancy saying? I mused silently, while in the pit of my stomach I felt the first twinges of nausea.

"Since Shelby is a pit bull, I'm afraid the officer, somewhat conditioned by a combination of reputation and stereotyping, compiled a generalized profile based on the behavior of a few dogs who may have strayed, letting fear get the upper hand. Joe, I took one look at Shelby and knew immediately she was neither nasty nor vicious. I knew she was in agony, malnourished and scared more of us than we should have been of her."

Nancy's recount left me speechless. Gazing down at my feet, I wanted to pretend I did not hear the awful words: *abused—malnourished—abandoned!* Vulnerable, Shelby was a defenseless puppy, willing to give unconditional love in return for some attention and respect. Yet, after having met her, there was no mistaking either the gravity of the situation or that Nancy's theory was anything but authentic.

The pit bull had all the signs and symptoms of a puppy that had been forced to endure agonizing torment. It was a shocking reminder of the evil nature of some human beings. Wringing my hands, I tried to be non-judgmental, though my instinct encouraged me to harshly condemn whoever had subjected Shelby to such torment.

"That's unpardonable," I blurted. "That's criminal!"

"I agree, Joe, but sadly there are many blood-curdling stories of animal cruelty and abuse. There are puppy mills all over the country where dogs are bred exclusively for mercenary reasons. No attention is paid to genetics and to the propagating of healthy animals. In other instances, the illegal practice of dog fighting makes sorry victims of non-aggressive pit bulls. These sweet-natured dogs, termed 'bait dogs,' usually get ferociously beaten in the ring because in lieu of defending themselves, they remain almost inert."

Shelby and I went through a long courtship.

Though I was far from naïve about the evils of the world, receiving confirmation from an experienced professional whose job description included animal cruelty cases escalated my nausea. I listened, not wanting to hear. While Nancy continued to speak about Shelby's brutal exploitation, a quote authored by Victor Hugo came into my mind: *"First it was necessary to civilize man in relation to man. Now it is necessary to civilize man in relation to nature and animals."* Apparently society has failed on both accounts, judging from the grievous abuse still inflicted on children and animals even in the twenty-first century.

"What happened when you took Shelby from the officer?" I asked, realizing at that point the puppy was at least safe from continued mistreatment.

"Joe, it was pitiful. Helpless and friendless, she cowered and shook like a weeping willow caught in a tempest, still unaware she had just awakened from a dreaded nightmare. I could see she was petrified. After all, I was another human being—the enemy. In her mind, why would I differ from those who had inflicted such torment on her? Although I tried to reassure her with soothing whispers, it was obvious Shelby now feared even unseen terrors!"

And then reality set in. Now that the haze had lifted, it was all quite clear in my mind. A feeling of anger mixed with devastation came over me. Much as I longed to uncover Shelby's secret, now that I had been successful, I wondered if I could ever get the broken puppy to bond with me. Would I be able to shatter the barriers built from months of abuse, heal her psyche and win her trust despite the trauma suffered at the hands of another or, perhaps, other humans?

My questioning continued—I had to know everything about the melancholy, mistreated pit bull who captured my heart the day I met her. I think it's called *love at first sight*—and I was smitten!

"Nancy, where did the name 'Shelby' come from?" I inquired. "Did she have an identification tag around her neck?"

"No, we christened her Shelby after the Shell station where we found her. Actually, that is how most of our dogs are named."

"I'd like to pursue a relationship with Shelby," I blurted, realizing I probably needed the patience of a saint to get through to her.

"I can see why, Joe. She's an engaging, beautiful dog."

Thanking Nancy for her kind concession of time and the wonderful work she does rescuing animals, I spun around and headed for Shelby's pen.

Walking across the shelter, I spotted my pit bull friend down on all fours, intent on licking her front paws. *Maybe she knows I'm coming to see her and she's getting herself ready. Isn't that just like a woman?* I thought, my lips parting in a broad smile.

As I neared the pen, Shelby ceased her hygienic ritual. Resting her head across her paws, she gave me a quick once-over.

"Don't let me interrupt your routine," I said teasingly. "I can wait until you're done. When you're ready, I'd like to take you for a walk."

Standing in front of her pen for several minutes, I realized Shelby had to be courted with the same romantic savvy and delicacy used to win the heart of a young, inexperienced princess. It was essential I make eye contact, but I had to be certain it would neither threaten nor intimidate her.

I waited for the right moment, certain a conquest was synonymous with a proper courtship. Patience rewards those who pay the virtue homage. Suddenly Shelby glanced at me, interrupting my thoughts. Drawing in my breath, I smiled. Despite the pain, despite the fear, despite her right to mistrust, Shelby's eyes twinkled with the illumination of two sparkling stars deeply set in a cloudless sky.

"This is a special dog," I whispered.

Shelby raised herself up unsteadily. My pulse raced. *Would she come to me if I called?*

First impressions are everlasting and, once made, can be neither retrieved nor revised. I could not make a mistake. One brisk movement, one misunderstood word, and my good intentions would be irretrievable.

"Hello, Shelby," I cooed softly. "I'm here to see you and take you for a walk." Again I paused, not wanting to insist. However, Shelby took a few suffered steps in my direction. Interpreting her gesture as an affirmative response to my request for a *date,* I slid down to her eye level, careful to be as graceful and gentle as possible, fearful I would scare her into withdrawing from me.

"Don't be afraid, Shelby," I whispered. "I just want to take a little walk with you—help you stretch your legs a bit."

Though there was no tail wag, something in her gaze assured me Shelby was agreeable. Excited, I slipped the leash around her neck, careful not to cause any additional trauma. This was a game of acute precision. Every move, every gesture, every word had to be part of a flawless strategy.

Synchronizing my pace to her limping stride, I escorted Shelby toward the gate. However, instead of crossing the threshold at the entry, she suddenly experienced a change of heart. Floundering a bit, she dropped down on her hindquarters. A thud, an echoing whimper, and Shelby sat immoveable.

"Are you in pain?" I asked, imagining how difficult it must be for her not only to walk on her seriously damaged hind legs, but to allow me, a representative of those who caused the injury, to accompany her. Obviously she vacillated between fear and wanting to think that perhaps my intentions in her regard were kind and loving. Trust is neither a gift nor an entitlement—it is an award that must be earned.

"That's okay, Shelby," I reassured, lightly passing the palm of my hand over the crown of her head. "I'll take you back to the pen. We can try again when you're feeling better." Interpreting her sudden hesitation as a reflex of anguish, I felt my stomach twist in knots. It was clear—Shelby was terrified of being hurt again. I read the trepidation in her eyes—they betrayed her secret. Nevertheless, there was absolutely no way I was giving up on Shelby! Once again, I prayed for patience.

My visits to the Bloomfield shelter became more frequent throughout the ensuing weeks. Though I loved all the dogs, and always had an affectionate caress and sympathetic word for each, I was seriously committed to courting Shelby. I studied new tactics, such as voice modification, and toned down my pitch to a softer, almost hypnotic level, hopeful she would feel more relaxed in my company.

"Shelby, I love you," I crooned as sweetly as possible without making a spectacle of myself in her presence. *It seems as if*

I'm pronouncing a declaration of love to my soulmate, I thought, chuckling silently.

Everyone responds to love—but would the abused and perhaps emotionally mangled pit bull puppy accept my friendship and compassion? Would she graciously receive and return my feelings of love? Before I could proclaim victory, I realized I had to be instrumental in helping Shelby overcome her issues of human mistrust and fear.

Taking into consideration the puppy's harrowing ordeal and resulting agony, I adopted a new approach—the dialogue. I started conversing with Shelby, speaking of my wife, children, family, pets and the 'guests' at the shelter. As I did with Fritz during my childhood, I discussed the various issues, events and challenges I was dealing with. Amazingly, she seemed to listen, rarely if ever tuning me out. Undoubtedly we were becoming acquainted with each other.

During one visit, several days after I had failed to get her to walk with me, I approached her pen, determined to overcome the reluctance she demonstrated earlier. I noticed her bowl was full, which explained why she looked so emaciated for her robust bone structure.

"Hello, Shelby," I greeted with a broad smile. The gleam in her eyes confirmed she recognized me. "Please join me for a walk today. Please don't say no! You can't enjoy sitting in the pen all the time. I'm sure you would like to stretch your legs. The exercise will help you heal more quickly."

Shelby was undisturbed by the earnestness of my request. Instead, studying me with her eyes, she inched closer. Did I dare assume I had gained points? Would she be willing to walk with me today?

Shelby, though not yet a year old, had already forfeited the innocence of puppy-hood, having experienced life more intensely than most dogs her age. In truth, she lived the dark, negative side of life, colliding with the evil nature of mankind, tasting the bitter

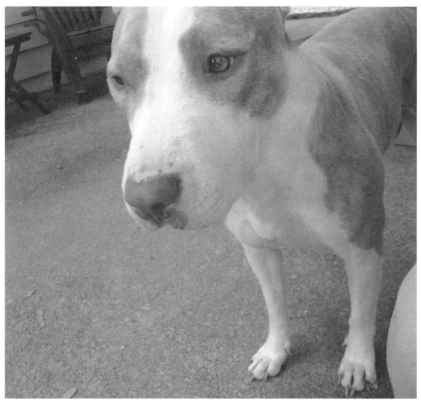

Slowly, Shelby accepted my friendship.

twang of pain, learning fear and withdrawal as a defense mechanism while developing an attitude of distrust.

Yet in spite of the almost certain criminal behavior to which she was subjected in her early months, Shelby was able to hold on to and develop that special trait shared by many dogs—the ability to distinguish between a well-intentioned individual and a ruffian with malicious intent. And notwithstanding the monstrous abuse, she never slipped into fear-aggression mode, like most wounded dogs or humans, for that matter, would have. Probably her trusted gut feeling reassured her she was in a safe haven, surrounded by people who wanted to love and nurture her.

In mid-March, two months after I had met Shelby, my patience began to bear fruit. From time to time, I was able to accompany Shelby on short walks, although the consequences of her mistreatment left her somewhat inconsistent in her behavior. Some days she would enjoy walking, and other days she preferred to remain undisturbed in her pen. Furthermore, I understood that the withering pain continued to condition her activity tolerance. The bad-day refusals and withdraws had nothing to do with me. By now she knew who I was.

Shelby and I were building a strong relationship, a bond based on mutual respect, love and credence in the reciprocal integrity between us, a relationship no different from the bond and camaraderie existing between people. It thrived on the same principles—it was all about the slow, steady beginnings of a lifelong friendship. I knew I was winning Shelby's heart.

Thorns and Thistles

"If all the beasts were gone, men would die from a great loneliness of spirit, for whatever happens to the beasts also happens to man."

—Chief Seattle of the Squamish tribe, in a letter to President Franklin Pierce

Lessons are learned through the experience of living, a practice that often involves walking in the shoes of another, feeling their emotions while thinking their thoughts. If we want to understand the significance and intensity of the human condition in all its nuances, if we want to develop patience and tolerance toward those who suffer, if we want to be unbiased in consideration, word and sensitivity, we must sense in our bodies, minds and hearts that very same hurt.

It is likewise in understanding those with whom we share the earth. No one aspires to standing before another to receive a verdict or even an observation based on a thought, a deed, a race, a faith or a condition. Why? Because, as humans, we cannot proclaim an infallible status. Therefore, error-prone as we are, the likelihood of rendering a false judgment is exorbitantly elevated. Additionally, the consequences can be deleteriously damaging.

Furthermore, reputations often are erroneously built on ignorance, a lack of valid criteria or a mimicked litany of assumptions
and repeated considerations authored by those knowing less than
we do. Then, unfortunately, these inaccuracy-ridden reputations
are used to generalize at the expense of others.

In all honesty, today, as a connoisseur of the effects of igno-
rance-fueled misjudgments, I beat my breast shouting, "*Mea culpa.*"
I was guilty of attitudinal blunders with respect to the opinions I
reserved for others, especially those in distress.

Revisiting the first twenty years of my professional life, I recall
some colleagues and employees mustering the courage to unburden
their deep, dark secret—a disease named anxiety and depression.
Young and inexperienced, I demonstrated neither compassion nor
understanding in their regard. In fact, I often brushed off their
laments and emotional misery as either situational dramatizations
or just plain character weakness.

Depression was not a *real* illness, I thought; it was merely a
transitory frame of mind crafted from disappointment, displea-
sure or a trying situation. Simply stated, it was merely a sporadic
unhappiness gaining dominance over a person's day. Therefore, I
was of the belief that when dark moments arose or when apprehension caused a sleepless night and morning exhaustion, it could
be alleviated with an uncomplicated remedy—get up, get moving
and continue with life.

"But I just can't get myself out of bed," one employee cried to
me one morning. "I can't make it to work—I'm not functioning
today. It is literally impossible." Judging his litany as a senseless
alibi for absenteeism, I questioned his words. Apathy sprang forward with increasing disbelief. *What nonsense was he feeding me
to justify and excuse his professional delinquency?*

I showed him neither compassion nor understanding, being of
the opinion he was merely slothful, irresponsible and inconsiderate of his position and the consequences his truancy exercised on
the business. But it didn't end there—this attitude was reserved for

all who indulged in similar lamentations. They were individuals using melancholy and a wish to pout at home to shun accountability. Never did I give the benefit of the doubt that perhaps the depression and anxiety they were dealing with was a very real medical condition—maybe even an illness.

Alexander Pope, in his *Essay on Criticism*, wrote, *"A little knowledge is a dangerous thing."* What wisdom! In reality a *little knowledge* is not far from ignorance, though a great more deleterious because it provides a false sense of security about our prowess in judging others.

Victims of calumny have paid heavily, be it generated from racial stereotyping or rumor, just as animals have been the unjust scapegoats of breed-profiling, often paying for man's error with their lives.

To the uninformed with just a slithering of knowledge, a person tormented by the ravages of depression is not sick but looking for an excuse to stay under the covers, whereas a pit bull trained to be aggressive or violent is representative of all pit bulls. The misleading notion that *"they are vicious animals and must be euthanized"* cut short the lives of many sweet, productive and loving dogs that would have made wonderful family pets.

However, to the well-informed, every human being and every animal is an individual entity and should be treated as such. No one, man or beast, should be defined or judged according to the reputation of another, for even documented repute has been proven errant. In synthesis, the presumption of innocence in all species must be honored.

I needed to learn—unfortunately, I was part of the uninformed, a man with a mere sprinkling of knowledge about anxiety and depression, a man who was treading on thin terrain. So God remedied my ignorance, making of me a well-informed, empathetic and compassionate man. First he summoned me to the deaconate in the Catholic Church then two years thereafter came *le coup de grâce*—the final blow!

In 2006, on Sunday, June 11, my wedding anniversary, I awakened, feeling as if a bucket of ice water had been repeatedly flushed
through a gash in my head. Trembling despite the late spring
warmth, I noticed a sudden tingling in my arms and legs, which
both disturbed and puzzled me.

I couldn't decide if my lower limbs—two lead beams—were
suddenly disconnected or just defiant to commands. My respira-
tion was labored, my breathing rapid and shallow, my heart racing.
I struggled to fill my lungs to capacity, failing with every strained
attempt.

True to my fear, thoughts of hopelessness, misery and despair
ran through the crevice of my brain. "I cannot go on. I'm losing
it!" I heard myself whisper, shuddering from the terror of physical
vulnerability.

A horrifying sensation of abandonment engulfed me. I was
no longer in control—no longer in my body! *Where was I?* Who
had invaded my body, imprisoning me, slipping such confining
shackles around my ankles?

What is happening? I thought, petrified. *What predatory virus
have I contacted?* Judging from the severity of my symptoms, I
concluded I required immediate medical attention.

Barely able to kick off the light summer quilt Geralynn had
slipped over the sheets days earlier to accommodate the approaching spring temperatures, I pulled my legs over the edge of the bed.
The room spun around like a carousel at the amusement park. A
kaleidoscope of blurred colors whirled in front of my face, forcing
me back down on the bed. Channeling my breathing into slow,
deep, steady breaths, I tried to get a grip on the situation. It was
totally useless—I had lost it.

Eventually, after asking the Lord's assistance, I staggered into
the kitchen.

"Geralynn, something is very wrong," I rasped, slumping
heavily to the kitchen floor.

"Joe, what happened?" she blurted. Her questioning eyes followed my dive down. "You look awful—and you're trembling!"

"I can't do it," I exclaimed with the unwavering bleakness of a man on death row. "I won't make it through the day. I don't know what is wrong with me but I feel lifeless—like a puppet. There is no way I can maintain my schedule at church this morning. I just want to crawl back into bed and huddle under the covers—maybe it will all go away in an hour or so."

Confused by my bizarre behavior, Geralynn tried to be supportive. "Is there anything I can do?" she asked. "Would you like me to take you to the ER?"

"No—I have too much to do today. I don't have time—I have obligations to fulfill."

Praying long and hard, I managed to stumble into the shower. Water was always purifying and healing—perhaps I would feel better if I let the warming spurt work its magic on me.

God only knows how I was able to get myself vertical, dressed and over to the church, where I baptized ten infants and delivered the homily during two masses. Returning home after thanking the Holy Spirit for the empowerment imparted, I was certain that following a nourishing dinner, a pleasurable conversation with Geralynn and our two children, Joseph and Jenna, and a good night's sleep, I would be rehabilitated from the mysterious malady.

Dreams are a necessary vehicle in the lives of men, women and children. They keep us fueled, optimistic, motivated and energized. However, some awakenings are the manifestation of a sometimes-bitter reality. Still, without dreams, hope hesitates and without hope, life becomes inert. I wanted to drift off and dream I was whole and in control.

The following morning, my eyes sprang open at the first buzz of the alarm. My limbs were dead weight again. I could barely catch my breath. My head throbbed. Enmeshed in an out-of-control wind turbine, I was wrenched in misery. A man of faith, I struggled to reconcile the mysterious unknown of my sudden 'illness.'

My descent into depression was fast and unexpected as well as physically and emotionally crippling. Every sunset brought the hope I would wake up whole and healed. Every sunrise confirmed I was grasping for an illusion.

Relating to Sylvia Plath, the author and poet who felt she was living life in a bell jar, I, too, felt compressed in the same receptacle, forced to perceive life as fuzzy distortions of what I once knew.

Was this my new reality? Some days were appalling and, willing or otherwise, I had little choice but to spurn my professional obligations. I was twirling out of control. Well over my head in melancholy, my constant companions were the anxious thoughts that took asylum in my head.

As I was unable to eat, my life-saving nourishment was several cans of Ensure a day.

I prayed. Realizing I was fighting a losing battle, I gathered my forces, plotted a course of action and confided in a dear friend that I was suffering from anxiety and depression.

"Joe, I know an excellent therapist. Let me set up an appointment. I'll drive you over if you want some company." Accepting his suggestion, I agreed to see Denise Rizzo, a wonderful woman and devoted professional imbued with the knowledge of a scholar and the patience of a saint. Denise took her commitment seriously; in consequence, she was instrumental in getting me to manage my depression and anxiety—not an easy task.

After several sessions and a detailed evaluation, Ms. Rizzo reached for her pad.

"Joe, I'm going to consult with a physician I work with and get you a prescription for some medication that will help minimize the symptoms of your depression and anxiety." *Medication, pills,* I thought, not very happy about having to swallow tablets on a daily basis.

"You must be conscientious and be certain to take the meds regularly as indicated," she cautioned, fixing her gaze on mine. The twinkle in her eyes told me she was on to me and my undefeated stubbornness. She knew my reluctance for pill-popping. "This is a real illness, Joe, with serious symptoms," she said calmly, "and, as such, needs to be treated."

My concentration wandered. *A real illness—a real illness! God was enlightening me. But did He have to do it in such a dramatic way?* I brought to mind my inconsiderate behavior with respect to trivializing the depression of others. How unfair I had been. Now in the shoes of a man suffering the same illness I previously made light of, I understood. The lesson was learned: *"Do not judge, that you may not be judged. For with what judgment you judge, you shall be judged..."*—Matthew 7: 1-2.

As aforementioned, Denise Rizzo's patience may eventually make of her a candidate for canonization. Just as she silently insinuated, I often failed to take my medication. Consequently, I had to live with aggravated symptoms. Despite my failings, Denise always exercised empathy in my regard, treating me with an advisory tone that was a distant cry from either angry or scolding.

Eventually, through trial and error, Ms. Rizzo was able to provide a medication schedule to suit my needs and obstinate nature. Cleverly, she weaned me off mega-doses of *Paxil,* a serotonin uptake inhibitor, and *Klonopin,* substituting a less aggressive dosage. This was the magic formula. I did, however, have to accept the truth—although depression and anxiety can be medically managed, they are recurring, chronic conditions.

While medication played and plays a role in the management of my disease, many days are truly challenging. However, with a great therapist, a loving wife and children and the most compassionate, faithful and understanding dogs imaginable, I was pulled from the brinks of disaster on numerous occasions.

Mornings are lethal, but to put fuel in an empty tank to get my motor roaring, I exercise regularly, eat healthy and attend to my personal hygiene routine, after which I focus on my dogs. Their need for love, attention and fostering are the sunrise in my day. Delighted to enjoy my company, they are well acquainted with the morning ritual and look forward to it with much animated tail wagging and wet, sticky licks.

Coffee brewed and safely poured into a mug, compliments of my best friend and loving soul-mate, Geralynn, I head for the couch, followed by my faithful, four-pawed companions. Silent, they wait as I pray, their big shiny eyes glued to my face. Each plays a part and has a designated spot on my person, which they honor every morning. No one invades the territory of another.

"Okay, let's get going. It's time to heal him. Let's get him going. This is what we have to do, so let's get on it!" is the phenomenal canine morning mindset. And, together with my devoted wife and children, Joe and Jenna, they do an excellent job, calming my anxiety, empowering my mind, energizing my body and lifting my spirit from the doldrums of depression.

Lessons are always learned as long as we have a heartbeat. Never underestimate or take for granted a dog's loyalty, nurturing and capacity for unconditional love—instead, treasure it, be grateful and, above all, reciprocate. It is a blessing.

Meeting of the Minds

"Until one has loved an animal, a part of one's soul remains unawakened."

—Anatole France

It was the end of March. Spring was fast arriving, making of winter's austerity merely cocktail-party banter. Tiny buds sprouted with the vaguest hint of color, offering reassurance that the landscape would soon be decorated with quick-to-bloom variegated flowers. The promise of regeneration in the air excited me.

Life was interesting, with its penchant for unpredictability and change, in spite of the challenges I confronted on a daily basis. With the awakening of every new season, the hope for revitalization and rebirth enthused my spirit.

Fueled by nature's stirrings and the encouragement of renewal, I slid out of bed, completing my morning ritual before schedule. Though anxious and depressed as dawn spread into morning, ever since I had first locked eyes with Shelby at the Bloomfield shelter, something in me felt altered. When in her company, my energy soared, lifting, even if for intermittent periods, my heavy heart.

There was a certain magic to the melancholy pit bull who had been made a victim of man's evil ways.

My prayer was that with the warmer, brighter days, enlivened by the animated echoes of yellow and black rails circling the skies, conversing among themselves, Shelby would be available to accept my company on walks. However, impatient to await a miracle, I refused to sit idle. Therefore, spurred to pursue the object of my delight, I headed over to the shelter.

"Joe," one of the volunteers shouted as I entered, "Shelby is waiting for you!"

At the mention of the sweet pit bull pup's name, the spring in my step heightened. *If only this reflected the truth,* I thought, heading for Shelby's pen. *If only she really awaited me to take her for a stroll!*

The prolonged sunlight assured me longer periods at the shelter and the ability to spend time with Shelby without neglecting my other four-pawed friends, who eagerly awaited my arrival and my company on their walks. Though their wet, sticky kisses were a delight to receive, my attentions were focused on the shy, withdrawn pit bull with the traumatic past. I had to break the ice. I had to win the heart of the 'girl' who played hard to get!

Weeks passed and like a faithful suitor refusing to accept defeat, I returned. With every encounter my feelings deepened— my desire to win Shelby's trust energized my days, giving me the boost I needed to live my own life.

Progress was slow but hope was unwavering and strong. Unexpectedly one day, a twinkle in her eyes betrayed a secret—Shelby recognized and acknowledged me! In that moment her gaze revealed neither traces of fear nor sadness.

As I neared the pen, her tail began to flutter every so slightly. Usually cocooned in a rather rigid demeanor, she seemed to have relaxed her guard. Was I truly inadvertently responsible for this slight but meaningful change?

From a faint flutter her tail danced into a sway—slow and

erratic as if uncertainty broke through her thoughts at given intervals. Perhaps Shelby was not fully comfortable opening her heart to me. I, on the other hand, was certain beyond reasonable doubt the ice was chipping. Happily, she did not entirely repress her feelings. The first baby step was taken.

On my next visit upon spotting my arrival, Shelby walked over to the gate. *Was she waiting for me to put on her leash?* My heart raced. *Did this mean she would accept my invitation for a walk?*

"Hello, Shelby," I said, encouraged by her friendly gesture. "Will you come walk with me today? It's such a beautiful day." Pausing, I held my breath. *Would she look away? Would she withdraw?*

I soon had my answers. Once on all fours, Shelby continued to fix her gaze on mine, slowly taking a step in my direction. She accepted my invitation—we had a date! Excited, I guided her out of the pen and into the sunny section of the yard. My heart was racing as I tried to inhale and exhale deeply to calm my tingling nerves. As we began to move, I heard a muffled whimper. I paused. Shelby paused.

"Don't worry, Shelby," I said, gently patting her head. "I'm your friend. I know you are hurting. That's why I want you to stretch your legs and get some exercise. It will make you feel better. Everything is going to be okay."

But everything was not okay. Shelby whimpered and limped in continuation. Observing her in the sunlight, I noticed how emaciated she was—undisputed evidence of insufficient nourishment. Her skeletal appearance in conjunction with the eternally full plate of food in her pen confirmed my theory. It was heartbreaking!

Saddened by her acknowledgment of pain, I led her toward a park bench poised in the quiet of the noon hour.

Seated, I controlled my urge to plant a kiss on her head, choosing conversation as a means of getting better acquainted. This had to be a perfectly orchestrated courtship. I had one chance to get it right. Delicate and fragile as Shelby was, any slip-up would ruin my chances. If I frightened her or led her to dislike or mistrust me, my quest for her heart would be forever forfeited. No negative suppositions were considered. I would not accept defeat.

Seated beside me, Shelby raised her eyes to mine—in anticipation. I knew I had to make conversation or I would bore my date to sleep. I could not deal with disappointment or, worse, rejection.

"Shelby," I began, "many years ago while growing up, I was befriended by a wonderful, loving dog. Fritz was my brother, my confidante and my best friend. We discussed everything from my parents and school to sports and girls. I even asked for his approval when I chose Geralynn to be my wife."

Despite her physical discomfort, Shelby sat still, listening to my every word. Occasionally the passing of another dog or the flapping of wings as several birds flew overhead momentarily distracted her attention.

Not to bring her to exhaustion, I escorted her back to her pen, pleased with the progress I had made. Undeniably I had made it to first base. Encouraged, I pursued further.

My trips to the Bloomfield shelter not only became more frequent but gradually extended for longer durations. By now it was common knowledge—I had fallen for Shelby! Trusting my intuition might have been a bit risky, leaving me open for disillusionment or unrequited love, but it was a decidedly better feeling than the teeth-chattering chill of apathy.

During our visits I noticed the presences of a certain synchrony. Whenever Shelby would relax and wag her tail, my anxiety and depression would wane. We seemed to be in harmony. *Was Shelby able to sense my state of mind? Was she tuned in to my flashing melancholy moods, just as I was open to hers? Did we share empathy for each other?*

Interested in this phenomenon, I dove into some animal behavioral studies. The surprising results confirmed my theory. Animals—dogs, in particular—suffered negative emotions just as humans!

I discovered that Martin Seligman, a psychologist and firm supporter of 'learned helplessness,' conditioned dogs to manifest symptoms of helplessness when placed in situations beyond their control in which they were powerless to flee. The consequential psychological stress resulted in bouts of clinical depression based on apparent defenselessness and vulnerability.

Therefore, according to Martin Seligman's experiments and results, and based on her traumatic history, Shelby was capable of suffering depression. This explained her sometimes back-laying ears, slightly narrowed eyes and the position I would find her in, with lowered body and raised front paws. Had I been an expert in canine body language, I would have immediately picked up on the signs of fear, anxiety and depression.

Despite it all, I pursued. Following a day's work as Vice Chancellor for administration for the Archdiocese of Newark, and responsible for many of the business functions, I would hardly see a day pass without some challenging issue or situation requiring untiring concentration and immediate attention.

Often, Shelby was my listening ear—my shrink. Available and willing, she was a loving, supportive presence as I worked through the issues. Never wavering in her direct eye contact, we sat face to face, like two individuals engrossed in discussing and perhaps resolving the world's problems.

"What's up, Shelby?" I asked one afternoon, taking her out to the bench. It was a calm, relaxing setting. She sat directly in front of me. At the sound of my voice she turned her head in my direction, not only establishing but holding direct eye contact throughout the conversation. This type of social behavior is rare in dogs, who, by nature, were afflicted with wandering attention spans at the drop of a feather. Instead, concentrated and focused, Shelby seemed to say—"Joe, I'm here for you. I'm listening to you. Feel free to unburden your heart and soul."

After selfishly monopolizing the *tête-à-tête,* I paused. *This visit is not about me,* I thought. *It's about bonding with my pit bull friend. It's about reassuring a scared, traumatized and hurting puppy that nothing of that heinous nature would ever befall her again.*

"Shelby, you're important to me," I blurted, feeling a rise of guilt over my burst of egocentricity. "I love you and I'm here to help you through this difficult time."

I hoped she would find support and comfort in my presence. Perhaps she lacked the insight to understand my intentions, but undoubtedly her intuition was as precise as a fine, well-tuned timepiece.

The feeling of a slight tickle on my hand caught me off-guard. *Was I mistaken in thinking a cool, humid nose had brushed against my hand? Had Shelby reached out to me? Was she declaring a reciprocal exchange of feelings between us?*

Amid the uncertainty and emotion of the moment, one thing was certain—the warm tear that drizzled down my cheek was not imagined! Leaning over, I kissed her gently on the head, always careful to eliminate any brusque gestures that could be misinterpreted as a prelude to aggression. I didn't want her to withdraw or recoil in fear. This was not an easy courtship. My desired *girl* was a very delicate and complex being. Each word and every strategy had to be flawless. There was no room for error—not with Shelby.

I walked Shelby back to her pen, filled her bowl with fresh, cool water, thanked her for her lovely company and promised to return the following day. Just as I lifted my hand from her face, thus erasing any trace of emotional attachment, a volunteer approached.

"Joe," he said, pointing to a couple several pens distant. "Becca and Paul are new to the shelter. Could you please show them around?"

"Sure," I said briskly, walking over, introducing myself and extending my hand in greeting to the pleasant-looking couple. In my opinion, anyone with compassion and the willingness to spend time with abandoned dogs was a person of substance, someone I could enjoy interacting with.

"If I'm not mistaken, I think they're interested in adopting one of our little friends," the volunteer whispered, barely loud enough for me to hear over the cacophony of various tonal barks.

A quick eye-check told me they would be wonderful canine

parents. I shifted from one foot to another, several times. I allowed the image of Shelby being adopted to drift reassuringly in my mind, across my doubts and my own personal feelings. But would Shelby be happy?

Balancing on the heels of my feet, I hesitated—just for a brief moment.

"I'd like you to meet Shelby," I stammered, taking a deep breath. "Let's walk over to her."

Agreeable to my suggestion, they trailed several steps behind me to her pen.

"Shelby," I said, "these nice people are looking for a dog to complete their family. Why don't you come closer so they can see how beautiful you are? *Tell* them you'd love to go home with them and be adopted. Then you can leave the shelter and have a place of your own."

A look reflecting disagreement and annoyance was aimed in my direction. I feigned nonchalance. "Shelby," I repeated, "come over here. I'd like you to meet Becca and Paul."

A pair of piercing, exasperated eyes ordered me to mind my own business. I persisted. Shelby took a few steps. I exhaled. Would she be gracious? Before I could ponder my question—it was answered.

With a thud, Shelby plopped down on all fours. Indifferent to the company at the door of her pen, she began a hygienic routine, licking her paws with vigor and unbridled enthusiasm as if they had been dipped in honey or some tantalizing nectar dogs find somatically irresistible. From time to time she glanced over at us with a lackluster gaze.

What was wrong? This was not my Shelby—the sweet, charming pit bull pup that had won my heart. It felt strange to look into her eyes and not see her. She was absent.

Becca and Paul had been investigated, cleared and given the green light for adoption. The Bloomfield shelter has a very strict and rigid adoption policy. Besides, clever and sensitive as she is,

Shelby had to sense they were warm, caring, well-intentioned people looking for a dog to love and nurture.

Maybe things were a bit more complicated with Shelby. Due to her trust issue, perhaps she needed more "get-acquainted time" to feel comfortable and reassured with Becca and Paul. Maybe if they came to see her a few more times, she would warm up and learn to trust them. So many maybes—but I had to hope. This could be a life-saving event for Shelby!

"Don't be discouraged," I muttered, "she's a lovely dog. She just needs more time."

"Okay," Paul said, turning to leave, "we'll be back in a few days."

After accompanying them to the door, I returned to Shelby. The look of wavering disdain and melancholy in her gaze told me she was not interested. But why? She had the opportunity to leave the shelter, have a home with a wonderful couple and be part of a loving family. Why would she turn her back on such a stroke of luck? Why refuse a blessing? Maybe my hunch was right—perhaps it was a question of time.

Stirrings
of the Heart

"The worst sin towards our fellow creatures is not to hate them, but to be indifferent to them. That's the essence of inhumanity."

—George Bernard Shaw

A lover of dogs and ravenous for knowledge regarding the 'animal condition' in a twenty-first century world, I took some computer time to browse various websites offering diverse information, much of which was not very enthralling. My efforts led me to a startling discovery that flushed my face red-hot. According to the HSUS, Humane Society of the U.S., animal shelters welcome an excess of six or seven million abandoned dogs and cats yearly!

I queried, *Why would anyone repudiate, let alone criminally mistreat, an innocent animal, a creature whose life purpose is to give unconditional love with no questions asked and nothing in return but food, water, a roof and a little attention? And why are many humans reluctant to understand the sadness and misery of animal rejection?* Helpless and vulnerable like children, dogs depend on man for survival. Though seemingly a flimsy statement, in reality it speaks a truth—all dogs have one possession, one gift from God: their lives…lives at the mercy of mankind.

Although the statistics are disturbing, the real devastation hides behind the fact that almost half of these abandoned creatures face euthanasia and not solely due to failing health. The problem is that in gaining an un-adoptable status, a dog faces an irrevocable capital punishment sentence, unless human love and kindness intervene to stay the 'execution.'

Interestingly, a California-based organization called Asilomar was instituted to investigate and alleviate the sorry plight of wonderful, healthy animals that would make excellent additions to loving families. Asilomar's mission is to work toward a goal focused on lowering euthanasia statistics by encouraging people to seek pets via animal shelters.

Therefore, when Becca and Paul returned to the Bloomfield shelter as promised, I was elated. Spotting them at the entry, my shoulders tightened. I eased my way over to greet them.

"Hi," I blurted, never seeking to camouflage my enthusiasm. "You're here to see Shelby?" Before a head nod merged into a verbal response, I interjected, "She's an amazing dog. She will bring you much joy, as she does to me whenever I visit her—just lifts me out of the doldrums!"

"Let's take another look, Joe," Paul said, following my lead towards Shelby's pen.

We walked over. As soon as I was in her view, my pit bull friend lifted her head. I prayed she would take it a step further and demonstrate some zest for her afternoon visitors.

Shelby, however, had a mind and heart of her own, irrespective of my wishes. From the corner of my eye I noticed the rudimentary signs of a rising diffidence! Maybe she was just a bit overwhelmed—maybe she was just awakening from a midday nap. Was I making excuses in vain? Was I denying reality?

"I think Shelby's a bit tired today," I stammered, trying to save the moment. An indulgent, animal-loving couple, Becca and Paul could be her lifesaver—her pass out of the shelter, her chance for family life! But why was she so sheepish and unassuming? Was

Shelby sending a message? If so, I had to know for sure. Her life could depend on this meeting.

"Hello, Shelby," Becca said sweetly.

"Come over here," I coaxed gently, believing or, rather, desperately hoping the mellifluous sound of my voice would reassure her she was not in harm's way.

The familiarity of my voice encouraged Shelby. Rising on all fours, she ambled over. To a specialist in canine body language, the analysis was easy. Precipitating from nonchalant and disinterested, her mood stopped at melancholy. A low, rigid tail, a fleeting, almost amnesic, glance and a reluctance to acknowledge the presence of her guests announced Shelby was not at her best.

"Joe," Paul said, shrugging his shoulders, "I think we'll pass on Shelby. Becca just told me her eyes are too sad—almost lifeless. I don't feel this dog will be a good fit for my family."

"Please reconsider," I blurted, fighting for Shelby as if she were the wrongly accused defendant in a criminal trial. "She's had a very tough beginning and needs some time to warm up to people. Won't you give her a chance? I know her now about three months and she's a truly sweet soul."

"No, Joe, I'm sorry. I don't think she's right for our family. The chemistry's not there. Besides, we don't want a gloomy dog."

I tried my best to counter their arguments, which, apart from all considerations, were unfair to Shelby. Undeniably she had her dark days, but she was certainly not wallowing in a slough of despondency, trenched or weighed down by an eternally dejected mindset. Hers were symptoms of post-traumatic stress and, I began to suspect, the manifestations of a strategically planned tactic. What was she scheming?

Fearful her feelings may have been hurt by Paul and Becca's critical remarks, I counteracted the urge to crawl into the pen and wrap my arms around her emaciated body with a loving look of solidarity.

"I'm sorry it didn't work out, Shelby," I crooned as soon as the couple parted company. My eyes moistened as I spoke. Was the hint of tears the result of sadness over Shelby's rejection? Or were they triggered by a deep-down relief my Shelby was still here for me? Was I being selfish?

Searching in the deep confines of my soul that evening, I was forced to admit I was petrified someone would hurt her again, either emotionally or physically—and what if I was no longer in her company to protect her? Breathing a sigh of relief, I drifted off to sleep, whispering, "Thank you, God. Thank you for entrusting Shelby to my care."

The following day I hurried through my scheduled appointments, leaving ample time at day's end for a longer visit with my pit bull puppy. Hurrying over to her pen in the late afternoon, I questioned the egotistical nature of my thoughts the previous evening. Flashing a guilty look in her direction, I greeted her with a strong, "Hi, Shelby—how are you doing today?" praying she would not show any signs of yesterday's rebuff.

Before I could extend an invitation for a walk, she was standing on all fours. An initial hazy light in her eyes brightened. There was neither fear nor sadness present in her gaze. Did I see a flicker of love?

I bent over to kiss her head. Shelby's mouth dropped open. Since the area was shaded and cool and she was not exercising, she was certainly not breaking into a pant. Therefore, without the slightest doubt, I knew in my heart Shelby was smiling!

When her tail lifted and broke into a wide, rhythmic sweep, the message was clear. Shelby did not want Becca and Paul to adopt her. That explained yesterday's diffident demeanor. Could it be Shelby was falling in love with *me*?

As my visits continued, I became increasingly mesmerized by the shy, withdrawn pit bull with the melancholy look. Our dialogues increased and by now she could have written my biography with all the fluctuations, mutations, revolutions, events and seesaw swings of my life, which, sadly, I had to admit were a great deal in excess of what I knew about her short, apparently tormented and tortured existence.

Though she gradually learned to trust me, her days were certainly not exempt from pain and anxiety. She had lived through a heinous experience, the after-effects of which were very pronounced.

"Shelby, I have three dogs at home, Rommel, Greta and Spartacus," I said during one of my visits. "Perhaps you can pick up their scent on me," I continued, extending my arm to position my hand directly beneath her nose. She obliged with several sniffs.

Encouraged, I pursued further, nervously gazing over my shoulder to check for eavesdroppers. "Rommel, Greta and Spartacus are part of my family."

Like a proud father boasting of his children's accomplishments, I told her a bit about each dog, hoping my enthusiasm would elevate her spirits.

"They know all about you, Shelby, and without even meeting you, they love you." Several licks later, I invited her for a walk.

Once in the garden, I noticed her limp was more pronounced. Every suffered step was accompanied by a soft whimper. Pausing, I hoped a brief sunbath under the mid-July summer rays might alleviate some of her agony. Instead the day's brightness revealed a series of deep, disfiguring scars etched on both hind legs—the testament to heinous crimes.

With my finger, I gently patted the large bald patches. They were like segments of a puzzle—a puzzle I would never be able to assemble. She recoiled a bit, whimpering softly, as if she tried to conceal her annoying discomfort.

Leaning over, I whispered, "Shelby, I wish you could talk to me about your past. I have so many questions. Who did this to you? What happened to your legs? I want so much to help you get well."

Leaving for several days, I bid my pit bull friend goodbye, uncertain if I would ever see her again. In her pitiful condition, she may not be alive upon my return. For a few fleeting seconds, I gazed in Shelby's direction. Eye contact made, I once again declared my love. Turning, I left the shelter as a tear ran down my cheek.

In my mind, I ploughed through a series of deplorable scenarios regarding what had happened to Shelby and what fate could possibly befall her in my absence. Would I ever see her again?

Throughout my short time away, I included Shelby in my evening prayers, asking God to protect this innocent creature from any further adverse experiences. She was certainly not born to be tortured!

Upon my re-entry, I returned to the shelter refusing to dwell on gloomy thoughts. However, with cautious optimism intermittently tangled in strands of pessimism, I headed for Shelby's pen.

"Hello, Shelby," I shouted, thrilled and relieved to see her. "I'm back!"

Observing her exaggeratedly frail body, my eyes clouded.

Who could possibly mistreat one of God's innocent creatures? I muttered under breath. *What motive could there be for lashing a dog?* It's true she was a pit bull and probably the unjust victim of breed profiling, but inflicting bodily harm on an animal is criminal.

When our eyes met, I was showered with deep sorrow. Despondent and pitifully downtrodden, my little friend was practically listless. It seemed as if she had abandoned herself to dying. More than likely she had misunderstood my brief absence, believing I had betrayed her.

I had to rekindle the relationship. I had to be certain I could gain Shelby's trust. Then again, why should she trust me after the atrocious torture she had endured as a tiny puppy? A human had tortured her, and I, too, was human.

"Is it about the agony of discrimination?" I blurted. "Shelby, were you beaten because of who others mistakenly or ignorantly thought you were?"

Frustrated and anxious, I kissed her head. "I'm back now. I'll be going on vacation in a couple of weeks with Geralynn and my kids, but I'll never leave you," I reassured.

Although witnessing her regression broke my heart, I felt she was sending me a message, brushing her cold nose across the palm of my hand. What was she trying to tell me?

On the way home, holocaustic scenes of a famished, frail and trembling Shelby, desperate and ruptured in spirit, flashed before my eyes without respite. "She's a living being," I thought aloud. "She deserves respect and dignity. She deserves love. Instead, deprived of all her rights, she is going to succumb. I have to rescue her or she will relinquish her life. This cannot be God's plan for Shelby!"

Driving home, I wept for Shelby, for her agony, even though I knew not what had really occurred. My tears oozed from a pained heart. I could not let the tormented pit bull down. Whether Shelby lived her life or whether she died was up to me.

My eyes dried, though filled with sadness, I regarded Geralynn at dinner.

"What's the matter, Joe? You look as if you have been crying," she asked, worried.

"I think it's an allergy," I muttered, uncertain how to breach the discussion about Shelby. But my demeanor was betraying my secret.

Discontinuous spells of insomnia and restless evenings rendered my own bouts of depression more intense. Images of my suffering, helpless pit bull friend haunted my waking and sleeping moments. It was time to make an important decision.

Though I always looked forward to family vacations as a joyous, loving experience and opportunity to spend quality time with Geralynn, Joe and Jenna, the seemingly hopeless plight of Shelby drew a curtain over my enthusiasm. Silence substituted conversation.

"Joe, what's wrong?" Geralynn asked, visibly worried. The history of my emotional condition is always a motive of concern.

"Don't you feel well? You seem down—has something happened that I don't know about?"

It was time. The scene was set. I had the attention of the whole family. It was now or never—but Shelby's life depended on it. We were enjoying a short drive before dinner.

Taking a deep breath, I told my wife and children about Shelby: her trauma, my visits, our walks and dialogues, as well as her alternating encouraging progress and oppressive setbacks.

"She's a beautiful, sweet dog," I said, fighting the tears. "Sadly, considering what little evidence we have to go on, Nancy, who rescued her, and I feel she was the victim of discriminatory profiling that categorized her as violent and unfit for family integration. Furthermore, based on her mangled hind legs and palpable scars, it is evident she was probably abused."

"How awful," Geralynn murmured, seconded by Jenna then Joe.

I finished my silent, short prayer for assistance, cleared my throat and lightened the pressure of my foot on the accelerator. Silence fell quickly, unexpectedly, inside the vehicle like a thick, dark cloud during a sudden, unpredictable tropical storm.

I afforded my wife and kids time to let their thoughts float freely and digest what I had just related. Instead of praying, I entered the atmosphere of silence, polishing the few lines spinning in my mind.

The car slowed. Several horns tooted. I veered gently to the right lane.

"I was thinking," I began, the echo of my three words calling everyone to attention. A peek in my rearview mirror brought a smile to my lips. Joe and Jenna abruptly relinquished their slouching positions. Did I really have that kind of power with young people?

"We are four people in this family," I continued, "two males and two females. We have three dogs—two males and one female. Perhaps it's time to invite another female in our family. In so

Shelby's eyes are windows to her soul.

doing, both genders will have equal representation. One pet per person—two males and two females. It is called balance and harmony. Therefore, based on the principle of equal representation, I was thinking that if everyone is in agreement, I'd like to adopt Shelby. I'd like to take her home to live with us!"

Because they were aware of Shelby's physical and emotional issues, which I openly shared with my wife and kids, there was bit of initial apprehension.

"Do you think Shelby will get along with Rommel, Greta and

Spartacus?" Geralynn asked. "Will they resent her? Will she be fearful of them?"

"They will love her—you will all love her as I do—you will see," I exclaimed, no longer caring to conceal my enthusiasm.

Understanding my attachment, empathy and heartbreak over Shelby, Geralynn agreed.

"Joe, Shelby is more than welcome to join our family!" An in-unison "yes" from the rear sealed the decision. I was delirious with joy.

The following morning, just two days prior to start of our vacation, I ran to the shelter to tell Shelby the news!

"Shelby, I'm going to adopt you," I screamed, darting over to her pen. "You will be coming home with me as soon as I return from vacation. But only if you want to!"

I don't know if my own euphoria kicked in, causing a mirage, but I was absolutely certain Shelby's eyes glistened, her front paws did a little rhythmic pit-a-pat as if she were dancing and I was certainly not mistaken about her swishing tail. Undoubtedly, Shelby agreed. She wanted to be a part of my family.

Upon my return from vacation, I scurried about, preparing a place for Shelby in my home. Rommel, Greta and Spartacus were lovingly informed of their new sister and reassured my love and attentions were unwavering, despite the new arrival.

The following day, after Sunday mass, I slipped off my dalmatic and, hardly able to breathe, I headed to the shelter to pick up Shelby. Once again—only if she was still in agreement!

Homeward Bound

"The assumption that animals are without rights, and the illusion that our treatment of them has no moral significance, is a positively outrageously example of Western crudity and barbarity. Universal compassion is the only guarantee of morality."

—Arthur Shopenhauer

It was unanimous—the entire family, human and canine, would make the journey to the Bloomfield shelter to accompany Shelby home. Everyone's enthusiasm was spontaneous and effervescent, and they had not yet made her acquaintance!

Reigning in my bubbling excitement, I decided it was best to make the short two-mile drive in two cars. This would be easier on Shelby and not create any unanticipated mishaps with Rommel, Greta and Spartacus. Though they were well-mannered and usually in possession of a superb knack of knowing how to coexist peaceably, I could not predict the reaction upon meeting their new sister and certainly did not want Shelby to have an unpleasant first impression of her siblings.

It was unthinkable that Shelby would endure any additional trauma; therefore, this fragile rescue mission was of the utmost importance. It was about the settling and burying of Shelby's anguish by providing a safe, nurturing environment for her to heal and enjoy life in the surroundings of a loving family—a right long overdue and unjustly sequestered.

Geralynn and I arrived first and waited for Jenna and Joe, who were just a traffic light behind. Since the shelter did not approve of other dogs roaming around, my wife and children remained outside with Rommel, Greta and Spartacus while I went to collect Shelby. Furthermore, I felt it would be less stressful for her to encounter the family in the parking area, as it was neutral ground for all. The idea was to provide as smooth and unruffled a transition as possible.

Upbeat and confident, I entered the shelter. Once in front of Shelby's pen, I greeted her with my usual gusto. "Hello, Shelby— today is the day. You get to meet the family I've been telling you about. We're all here to take you home. It's over—you will never be alone again!"

Although there is much speculation regarding the extent of an animal's ability to understand human emotion and communication, in Shelby's case it was obvious she knew exactly what was happening.

Bright and glistening, her eyes followed my every move, never leaving the contours of my face. As she shuffled back and forth on her hindquarters, her tail completed several broad sweeps before she stood and walked over to where I waited, leash in hand.

Excited, my hand clumsily collared her as she wiggled and squirmed in delight like a small child dressing to go out and play. With a racing heart, I led her toward the gate and her new life.

Spotting us, Geralynn and Spartacus jumped from the car, a gesture quickly imitated by Jenna, Joe, Rommel and Greta. The welcoming committee was at attention and ready to greet the new arrival. The energy was electrifying.

Hesitant at first, Shelby fixed her gaze on me, perhaps for reassurance. Smiling, I patted her head. "They are all here for you, Shelby," I said. "They love you."

"This is Shelby," I said, doing the introductory honors.

"And, Shelby, these are your brothers and sister, Rommel, Spartacus and Greta."

Standing timidly, she waited as her siblings edged over, giving her the "sniff over." Meanwhile, human silence permeated the quiet, interrupted exclusively from time to time by the echoes of nature.

Immobile, I prayed the initial interaction would be friendly in a non-overtly aggressive manner. Dogs sometimes bubble over with excitement, crouch down and abruptly raise their front paws in the face of the desired companion. While the behavior signals acceptance and a willingness to play, I feared Shelby might misinterpret the exuberant gesture and recoil in trepidation.

My prayer was not only heard but apparently well received. Rommel, Greta and Spartacus approved of what their olfactory senses revealed. Shelby's scent did not betray her gentle soul. Breathing a sigh of relief, I watched as the pit bull pup returned a few sniffs. The energy was powerful. Tails pointed to the heavens, wagging in unison. It was official—Shelby was accepted by her canine brothers and sister!

"She's beautiful, Dad," Jenna said, bending over to give Shelby an affectionate pat on the side of her face. My children were well versed in the science of animal behavior, having been instructed from an early age to be certain a dog always had full view of every hand movement. This would prevent any abrupt defensive-aggressive behavior based on the assumption of inevitable harm.

"We can see the attraction between you and Shelby," Joe chirped. "She has such a sweet look about her."

Of course, Geralynn was in full agreement with the children's comments, having met the pit bull pup previously during one of our visits to the shelter. Needless to say, everyone loved Shelby. Although I never doubted she would incontestably win their hearts, human and canine, it was enthralling to have the confirmation.

"Dad...Jenna, Spartacus, Greta and I will head for home," Joe announced, pulling open the door of his vehicle. "We'll see you there in a few minutes."

"Okay, I'll get Rommel and Shelby in the car and we'll follow you."

Geralynn opened the rear door and Rommel jumped in. Pausing, she glanced in Shelby's direction.

"Come on, Shelby, get into the car," she coaxed invitingly, slapping her palm on the seat a couple of times to reinforce the invitation.

With an intense gaze, Shelby's eyes rotated from my face to Geralynn's—eyes that spoke not of fear but frailty. Did she not understand? Was meeting the family perhaps too overwhelming? Was it asking too much too soon?

"Maybe she's a bit intimidated," Geralynn blurted. "I don't think she wants to get into the car."

Inflexible, Shelby sat unruffled like a career sentinel standing guard at the entrance of a palace. If her demeanor pointed to lethargy and indifference, her suffered glance revealed the predicament.

"Geralynn, I don't think Shelby is afraid or intimidated," I said softly. "She can't jump like the other dogs because her wounds are too serious. I think she needs help getting into the car."

Gently walking my newly acquired puppy to the vehicle, I lifted her, careful not to add additional injuries to her maimed hind legs. Once inside, a warm, moist nose brushed against the back of my hand, filling my eyes with tears. Shelby had expressed her thanks.

"My poor Shelby," I whispered, "who did this to you?" Who could have possibly been so malicious and pitiless to inflict such torture on a helpless puppy? Much as I knew I would never have the answers, I was certain I would never stop posing the questions.

Once she was comfortably inside the car, I hurriedly slid behind the wheel, buckled my seat belt, flashed a smile in Geralynn's direction, inflated my lungs beyond comfortable capacity and headed for home.

"Everything is going to be okay. Shelby has a home and family and plenty of love," I said. "Her misery is over. Now, if we can just encourage her to forget the horrors and begin anew."

Knowing all the nurturing and kindness would not alleviate the nightmarish memory, I still vowed to give it my best effort. Condemning the evil that had battered her so badly, I vowed to give Shelby the life she deserved. It was the first day of the rest of her life, a beautiful Sunday, August 10—a turning-point date that would be remembered and celebrated each year as her birthday!

Pulling up to the house, I realized the difficult part was just unfolding. How would Shelby adjust to her new life? Would Rommel, Greta and Spartacus exercise patience in her regard? Would their behavior be polite and considerate, in keeping with the family policy? Would she finally experience some of the happiness God brought her to life to enjoy?

Amid the questioning, one thing was assured—I would do my best to see her tail wag and her lips part in a smile. She was a member of my family now and, as such, entitled to all the benefits and perks available.

For a brief second I wondered if I'd have to persuade Shelby to get out from the auto. This was a new experience and I had to adapt instantaneously to the situation at hand. Unknowingly, I was in for a surprise. As soon as I opened the rear door of the vehicle, Shelby bounced right into my arms. If by chance I would have had a minute morsel of doubt regarding the adoption, it immediately vanished in the late summer breeze.

"Welcome home, Shelby," I exclaimed, gradually lowering her to the ground.

We walked around the property before heading to the backyard, where the family eagerly awaited her arrival. Rommel, Greta and Spartacus stood their ground, conscious of Shelby's presence in their lives but willing to demonstrate their "good upbringing."

I was somewhat concerned about Spartacus's customary "king of the realm" supremacy, but he seemed docile and gracious. He had the gallant manners of a lord meeting a lady for the first time.

Once again the sniff fest began among the four-pawed siblings; this time, however, Shelby participated. No one growled or barked. No one jumped or withdrew. I breathed a sigh of relief.

"Joe," I said, addressing my son, "I'd like to give Shelby a bath before we take her inside."

"Wouldn't that scare her, Dad?"

"Not if we do it in a slow, gentle way. She might even enjoy it. It's really hot today, and the cool water running down her back may be refreshing."

A look in her direction told me Shelby was possibly open for a new experience. Seizing the moment, I led her over to the water hose, explaining en route exactly what would transpire. Running through my mind was the ever-present fear of unconsciously causing any additional trauma; consequently, every word and action on my part was carefully measured and studied. As always, there

Her first day at our house.

Rommel, one of our doxies, is behind Shelby.

was absolutely no room for blunders because some blunders cannot be undone.

But water signified purification and healing. Actually, in the Catholic faith, water sanitizes the soul from the remnants of original sin. In all the baptisms I performed, infants and converts were rinsed clean from the stain of the first evil deed, and reborn into the grace of God and a new life.

Additionally, blessings are given and a certain protection from Satan's malicious reign of wickedness is offered either through immersion or the sprinkling of holy water.

In other spiritual spheres, cold and water are both yins and in combining the two, the resulting yin-yin equation is said to rinse out negative energy. I liked the symbolism and hoped that in washing Shelby, she would experience a rebirth. It was worth a try and if she cringed or sprang back, I would just turn the hose away from her.

Shelby stood next to me, eyeing my every move. With slow, steady hand movements, I turned on the hose and paused, watching as the slender, clear stream glistened in the sunlight. Shelby seemed mesmerized. Leisurely I sprayed her front paws then moved along to the rear. Licking her soaked paws, she seemed unfazed by both the sound and wetness of the water.

Courageously I let a spray of water trickle along the contours of her back, from her neck down to her tail. She stood motionless. Was she really enjoying the shower?

"Dad, I think she likes it," Joe said, surveying the scene. "Let's try it with some shampoo!"

Amazingly Shelby loved the bath, either for its cooling effect on a hot August day, or because, as I like to surmise, she enjoyed the cleansing and washing away of her devastating past. Sliding down on the grass, she rolled over, legs in the air, exposing her tummy to the refreshing sprinkle of cool water. I was eager to oblige. In a sense the water was her baptism into the new family.

Once showered and dried, I walked her inside the house. Uncertain of the indoors, Shelby did not budge from my side. Apprehensive of her new surroundings and the individuals, human and otherwise, in her life, she was somewhat hesitant to relax. Since I represented familiarity in a world of strangers, she kept her gaze glued to my face. Too excited to unwind, I could not entice her to ingest any food. It was understandable, considering the history.

That evening I escorted Shelby to her pen in my office, which was where all the dogs slept, each in their own spacious wired enclosure. To reassure her throughout the night, when my actual presence would not be visible, I gave her one of my t-shirts to sleep on as a kind of security blanket. I continued this ritual indefinitely, especially during the times I was absent from the house for longer periods.

With the rise of a splendid fuschia sunset the following morning, Shelby awakened, reborn. Miraculously, her transformation was an exhilarating testament to the healing power of love. She had an air of serenity about her that was utterly phenomenal and an acclimation rate I would assume was a record-breaker.

The sole worrisome issue was her poor appetite during the

Shelby resting at home.

initial days. It was comprehensible as she probably questioned the feelings of her newly acquired siblings. Would they accept her? Would they test her? Would she fit in?

Thankfully, the period of dubious thinking was short-lived. By week's end, Shelby was not only taking in nourishment but visibly enjoying her meals.

Rommel and Greta were wonderful, loving siblings with

whom Shelby bonded immediately. Spartacus, an extremely bright dog, feared he had to set the ground rules or risk forfeiture of his leader-of-the-pack status. However, genteel and gracious, though firm in his resolve to rule the kingdom, he let his new sister know through a series of pertinent, no-nonsense barks that he would be warm and loving, though she was to respect him as the boss.

A gentle lady, Shelby had not the slightest intention to dethrone her brother. She enjoyed the interaction and game-playing as part of the pack. Furthermore, happy to be rescued from the loneliness of canine foster care, she was thrilled to be a member of such a wonderful, nurturing family.

In her gut, Shelby knew her reprieve was a very special blessing. And, of course, she was deliriously charmed by and hopelessly in love with her dad.

A Life
for a Life

"An animal's eyes have the power to speak a great language."
—Martin Buber

A mazingly, in just a short time, Shelby was beautifully integrated in the family nucleus, interacting happily and effortlessly, dually with her human and canine siblings and her adoring parents. She was the beneficiary of love and nurturing, and her appetite bloomed, allowing her to consume nourishment in the same voracious way as her other three canine siblings.

With the passing days, I noticed that Shelby's skeleton, no longer visible to the naked eye, was concealed behind a thin layer of fat-fortified skin, canceling all traces of life-threatening mal-nourishment. From day one my commitment was to restore her well-being and in so doing I tried to eradicate any and all traces of injury and trauma.

Enjoying the company of Rommel, Greta and Spartacus, the pit bull pup required little if any coaxing to join them in play. Soon it appeared as if her accommodating nonchalance was ingrained from birth, instead of being newly acquired. A willing accomplice in their many activities, she scampered after the others despite her painful injuries.

I, on the other hand, continued to battle the demons causing havoc in my life. Discrediting the fact that part of my dilemma was my reluctance to adhere to my medication schedule, I sought other solutions to alleviate the heavy darkness that enveloped my body and mind. Summoning my faith, I believed it a worthy ally in the fight to conquer the depression and anxiety that held me captive in a tight-knit cocoon. Consequently, I continued to adopt a rather fruitless *laissez-faire* approach at various intervals with respect to managing my medication, until a cold, bitter misery expanded to overwhelming dimensions, forcing me back on track.

Mornings were a challenging drudgery. An array of bludgeoning symptoms left me fighting just to kick off the covers. I remember one instance among many. Looking back, it still entices chills to race up and down my spine.

One morning, offering a short prayer for strength before I left my bed, I slowly placed both feet firmly on the ground. Rising leisurely, I felt the lead apron that physicians and dentists use to protect patients against radioactive imaging fallout tighten around my chest and back as I inhaled. Though I had never lost hope, it was forever with me like second skin. *But would I be able to tolerate the heaviness another day?*

The lead vest, my uniform, shielded my body from brightness and the lightness of life. One size and one color, it 'dressed' me from morning until evening in all four seasons, never, ever fraying or wearing thin.

This phantom garment, with its weightiness anything but spectral, was an article of attire in my psychological wardrobe—an invisible item of clothing otherworldly in nature. I could neither loosen nor remove it for relief.

Unfortunately, on this particular day I had awakened more tightly trussed in the apron. Recognizing the sensation, I felt reassured I was not in the throes of a full-fledged heart attack, though my pulse rate spiked as I staggered out of bed. The pre-dawn silence in the house rendered my thoughts far too ear-piercing.

Therefore, listening to my melancholy brainwaves was not an option. They were there and stronger than my power of resistance. Any confrontation would have merely sent me boomeranging, exhausted, back under the covers. However, not a defeatist by nature, I polled my alternatives. A large percentage went to reaching for my medication.

The inertia and constricting feeling around my chest made it almost impossible for me to see past the sunrise. What was the purpose of continuing—it was all far too catastrophic. Although I believe deeply and unconditionally in the power of prayer, I was not connecting.

Has God forgotten about me? Am I that worthless as a human being? I whispered, gasping for air as the lead apron tightened. It seemed as if someone was tugging at it from behind, trying to suffocate me.

Drenched in the stifling complexity of my malady, I was certain not even my morning prayer, exercise and time with my dogs would ease the terrible feeling of doom hanging over me. All I wanted was a respite from the anguish and the annihilation of my existence.

Inertia controlling my body, I shuffled into the bathroom. There was no way I could possibly be productive that day. Just to maintain my breathing rhythm would be a miraculous achievement. On the other hand, if I ceased to breathe—if I existed no longer—I would be freed from the dark demon's clutches. I would no longer feel hopeless and incompetent, trapped in a lethargic body, girdled in a cumbersome lead vest. *Was that the answer? Would that put a definitive end to this nightmare?*

Ugly thoughts careened out of control, trampling on my reasoning, quashing my conscience. Desperate alternatives, rather attractive in my desperation, overstepped moral boundaries. On the other hand, what was the point of prolonging this agony?

Standing in front of the medicine cabinet, I grabbed two vials of pills, intentionally avoiding catching my reflection in the mirror. *Was I afraid of eye contact? Was I attempting to evade the truth?*

I knew better: *Thou shalt not kill.* My conscience was betraying my body. Resisting the spiraling self-destructive thoughts, I ran to the gym for my morning workout. Exercise was beneficial for body and soul. Usually the surge of endorphins would rev up my motor, powering me for a day's living. *Would it work today?*

Designing and maintaining a physically and mentally active plan was advantageous. It kept me on my feet even if, most of the time, I was teetering along the edge of a precipice. Determined, I went through my cardio routine.

Afterward, I showered, dressed and headed for my office. Waiting for me were issues to resolve, voice messages to answer, people to meet and discuss with and strategies to plan. Nothing seemed gainful: not the fervent prayers to a merciful God, not the presence of my loving dogs, not the exercise or martial arts movements I tried as a last resort—nothing—not even the dive into professional obligations. I was shackled and shoved into an impasse, unable to untangle the chains.

Nothing resonated in my mind. I couldn't concentrate; consequently, I had no ability to focus. Realizing it was counterproductive to remain at work, I headed for my car. Seated behind the steering wheel, I knew I had to step into the role of therapist. I had to be both patient and analyst. It was about devising a solution and successfully convincing myself of its merit. I guess it could be called an auto-pep rally—a gathering with myself for the purpose of self-preservation through self-motivation and personal empowerment.

The effort paid a minus dividend. I failed miserably. Pulling into the driveway, I tottered into the house. There was only one solution!

Once in the bathroom, I hurriedly grabbed the Clonopin, turned on my heels, avoiding a mirrored confrontation with myself, and walked to the bedroom. As I gazed down at the capsules, my mind orchestrated a scenario in which I was no longer. For a fleeting moment I entertained the idea of my own demise. It brought relief.

"This is no way to live...this is no way to live...this is no way to live, I chanted over and over, like a pluri-syllable mantra, pausing only to breathe when I felt my lungs would explode. Lowered, my gaze was fixed on the vial of pills. As I stacked the medication, my thoughts took a twisted detour. *What if I ingest all the medication, slide into bed and pull the covers over my head? It would cancel the pain once and for all.*

All I had to do was 'push and turn,' as instructed on the cap, load my mouth and swallow a glass of water. It was so easy, too easy—easier than getting up every morning, easier than dealing with the expired battery within, the battery I could no longer recharge. This was the real deal. Desperation had gained mastery over my body and mind.

Geralynn was at work, Jenna in school; Joe was occupied in class with his students and I had no inclination to phone my therapist, Denise. Except for Shelby, Rommel, Greta and Spartacus, I was alone in the house. A flicker of rational thinking amid the irrational thoughts left me intentioned to set my desperate plan in motion. A sudden deafening stillness swaddled my shoulders.

No one would violate my plan for serenity. No one would be confrontational with respect to my decision. No one would trespass on my free will. No one would try to halt my desperate attempt for a respite from the agony that was consuming me day by day without a truce. Instead they would understand why I had little choice but to end it. God would understand—He would forgive me! Would He? But one of the Ten Commandments entrusted to Moses said, "Thou shalt not kill."

My mind supposed I was already dead, shattered under an iron curtain that would not lift regardless of how much I tried and how long I prayed. It seemed as if my implorations kept rebounding off empty, echoless walls. I gave it my best. I tried every option. I took every medicine prescribed—all to no avail. Suffocating from depression enabled from anxiety, I could not find the energy to survive, let alone fight and overcome. Therefore, opening the vial, I succumbed to a momentary human frailty intensified by the wave of desperation that washed over my head.

Then in His very own unique and mysterious way, God intervened.

Pausing, I placed the vial on the nightstand, and it suddenly hit me. *I cannot go without saying goodbye to my beloved dogs. I owe them an explanation and a respectful farewell for closure!*

Rising from the bed, I felt the floor tremble beneath my already unsteady stride. Drawing a deep breath, I headed into my office a broken and desperate man, seeking my canine family for one final goodbye.

"Hi, Rommel, Greta, Spartacus—hi, Shelby," I stammered, my eyes moistening. I walked over to where they stood, each gazing at me with a puzzled expression. Kneeling, I extended my hand, patting each one on the head.

"I love you," I whispered, my voice crackling like a pubescent fourteen-year-old boy slipping in and out of a testosterone storm. Hugs and kisses followed the declarations of love. One by one, I addressed them—first Rommel, then Greta then Spartacus, who, having been abruptly awakened from his afternoon siesta, was still stretching and somewhat groggy. But just for a quick second.

Large, glistening eyes, wagging tails and erect ears communicated reciprocity. The gratification and sheer splendor of requited love! But it did not end there. What about Shelby?

My internal tracking device told me this was going to be beyond excruciatingly anguishing. *How would I say goodbye to Shelby? Could I?*

Approaching the sofa where she reclined, I dropped down on my knees, establishing eye contact with my beloved pit bull puppy. Extending my arms, I placed my cupped hands under her chin, cradling her head. Bolstered by her soft, compassionate gaze, my heart raced.

"*I'm here,*" her sweet expression said. Her loving whimper took it further. "*You're okay, Dad—I know it's hard. But you can make it. This is why I'm here. This is what the crossing of our paths means. This is why we met!*"

Jolted by her uncanny sense of unfolding drama, I realized what had just happened. *Would Shelby survive another abandonment? Would she understand why her beloved "dad" no longer played with her, no longer fed her, no longer was a presence in her life, offering love and nurturing?*

Empathetic and compassionate due to her own traumatic ordeal, Shelby freed her head from my grasp, never breaking the eye contact that linked us. Moving closer, she licked the tears streaming down my face with an understanding heart. Once again her whimpers and pleading glance told me she loved and needed me. *Everything is going to be okay, Dad. I'm here for you now, just as you are for me!*

Miraculously, I believed her. My conscience awakened. Ashamed and relieved, I contemplated what had almost happened. *What was I thinking? What was I doing?*

Terrified of what could have been, I encircled my arms, covered with goose bumps, around Shelby, rested my head on her back and wept. Motionless except for her rapidly beating heart, she not only comforted me with her loving presence, but gave me the reassurance that my purpose in life was manifold.

I was here to administer—my family—my flock—my pets and, of course, my beloved Shelby, whom I had rescued. They loved and needed me—she loved and needed me. Believing in the sanctity of life, human and animal, I realized how close to the edge I had come. Dangling dangerously from the precipice, I felt a splintering remorse.

Uplifted and momentarily undressed of my lead vest, I invited the dogs for a walk. The synchronized tail-wagging and paw-shuffling confirmed they knew the crisis was over.

But Shelby did not leave my side. Perhaps she was not quite sure of her healing powers. As we stepped outside, she rubbed up against me several times, a gesture canine behaviorists define as the act of hugging.

"Thanks, Shelby," I whispered, convinced she truly understood my plight. "You were sent here for a reason. You saved not only my life—but my soul. You are an angel."

Amazingly, God chose one of His purest and most innocent creatures as His emissary—not a child, but a puppy. Apparently Shelby came into my life for a reason—she was saved because God had a plan for her. This was not just about my rescuing an abandoned, abused dog from a shelter. This was about my salvation and Shelby's very special mission.

As I leaned over to give her a kiss, our intentions crossed midway. Suddenly I felt her warm, moist tongue brush against the tip of my nose.

"Shelby, you and I have come full circle."

Shelby's Purpose Revealed

"Hear our humble plea, O God, for our friends the animals who are suffering; for any that are hunted or lost or deserted or frightened or hungry...We entreat for them all Thy mercy and pity, and for those who deal with them we ask a heart of compassion and gentle hands and kindly words. Make us, ourselves, to be true friends to animals and so to share the blessings of the merciful."

—Albert Schweitzer

Numerous and diverse are the images of angels in the human imagination, images from lithe-bodied, rosy-cheeked individuals with wings and luminous halos highlighting flowing, honey-colored tresses to sweet, four-winged, tousle-headed cherubs barely able to assume an upright position.

In sync with my own mind's eye is the concept of a four-pawed, tail-wagging angel on a leash. Intending no disrespect for the angelic hierarchy, I am aware the Lord engages other species as His messengers. After all, the gift of giving love, compassion, empathy and companionship welded to the ability to bring comfort and healing does not pertain exclusively to human beings.

Perhaps my love for animals conditioned my thoughts—perhaps not. Maybe my visualization of the angelic hierarchy was somewhat unrealistically formatted—maybe not. I was visualizing canine angels.

Was I lost in some mythological fairy-tale realm? Or was I one of the privileged few willing and able to appraise all living beings, attributing merit when due regardless of a creature's species? And why should animals be excluded from the 'roster' of kindhearted heroes and doers of good? Somehow I knew better. Call it a seventh sense or whatever. It truly matters not.

As days rolled into weeks, I noticed Shelby was having difficulties reaching the sofa and chairs. More precisely, she needed help joining Rommel, Greta and Spartacus, comfortably curled and nestled beside me. Moreover, her stride seemed lopsided and somewhat wavering at times, especially when a busy schedule zapped her energy at day's end.

Though I knew she had been hurt, I had not even an inkling regarding how serious her wounds were. Observing her on a daily basis, I was shocked to notice her rather severe handicap status. Frustrated, she tried her best to keep pace with the other dogs, probably unwilling to disappoint and/or worry me.

However, the suffered movements, the interrupted mobility due to stiffened joints and the muffled whimpers sent a red light flashing. Shelby was in pain!

"Joe," Geralynn called, interrupting my thoughts. "It's such a beautiful evening. Why don't we take Shelby and go for some ice cream? I'm sure she'll love the ride."

I had to admit it was a very enticing suggestion. Though a balmy mid-September day, a cooling breeze rendered it inviting to be outdoors after sunset.

"Sounds like a great idea," I blurted. "I'll get Shelby's leash."

Since Joe and Jenna were at home to give company to Rommel, Greta and Spartacus, the moment was opportune. There was no way we could have calmly managed four dogs at an ice cream shop filled with kids and other dogs. Besides, Shelby needed the diversion to distract her from the physical woes making her life a difficult trek.

I parked and we exited to get the frozen yogurt. The setting was perfect—children running about frolicking and animated sounds of life being lived. It was an ideal setting for Shelby to get a glimpse of the real word.

Once I helped her out, Shelby seemed to enjoy stretching her legs and being out in the late summer air. Consequently, I thought it best to prolong the outing. Adjacent to the ice cream shop there was a beautiful park. Usually bustling, it offered adventure for dogs and kids. I was certain the still-verdant grass, lush and soft underfoot, would be a delight for Shelby.

"Let's take a little walk," I suggested to my wife. "Are you up for it?"

"Sure," Geralynn responded. "What about Shelby? Do you think she would like to join us?"

"Let's ask her and find out," I quipped coyly, "though I do not want to leave her alone in the car. It might frighten her or rekindle bad memories."

At the sound of her name, Shelby sat up at attention, her ears erect. The "ready for action" demeanor together with the sparkle in her eyes shouted, 'Count me in.'

"Well, I guess we have the answer," Geralynn said, smiling, giving her a quick pat on the head.

Dogs need socialization and the opportunity to familiarize themselves with the world around them. Although, at home, Shelby interacted with her family—human and canine—I believed she should develop a better feel for strangers, children, traffic, other dogs and the sounds of a lively environment. Like children, puppies should be acclimated to their surroundings and feel secure when away from the all-too-familiar residential milieu.

With Shelby's story still a dark unknown except for the history built on her scars and wounds, I was prepared for the worst-case scenario. Therefore, realizing that any hesitancy or withdrawal on her part was undeniably a corollary of the abuse endured, I wanted her to feel as comfortable and at ease as possible in any setting. Perhaps the memory of torture could be substituted by new pleasurable experiences and loving gestures in her regard. It was in a sense like reeducating a waking coma patient. But it was worth a try.

Explorers on a quest to conquer new territory, Geralynn, Shelby and I headed in the direction of the park. Even if her tread was far from brisk, she kept pace with our measured strides. Lifting her head just high enough to catch a gentle breeze, she doted on the cooling puffs of air caressing her face.

Geralynn's gaze met mine. Our smiles were reciprocal reflections. How pleasing it was to see our sweet puppy enjoying a moment of pleasure, especially after all she had been through—both the known and the frightful unknown.

We were about a half-block shy of the park at the specific location in which two senior housing complexes stood overlooking the flora and those men, women, children and dogs who were blessed to stroll through, savoring and participating in the beauty of nature. Though a panorama definitely not scattered with primrose, it represented a vision of serenity to an observant eye.

Nearing one of the buildings, I noticed a wheelchair-bound gentleman of a certain age seated in front, witnessing life unfurl before him. Realizing that perhaps some individuals, especially those somewhat physically infirm, may feel intimidated by the proximity of an unfamiliar dog, I shifted direction, moving Shelby to my left while distancing myself just enough to ensure a safe passage.

"Hello," the gentleman greeted, flashing an ear-to-ear smile as genuine as a one-hundred-dollar bill newly released by the Federal Reserve. "What a beautiful dog you have! Can you bring her over? I'd really like to meet her!"

Though thrilled and proud of my pit bull pup, I was abruptly thrown off-guard. Reconciling myself to the good sense of exercising restraint, I hesitated, somewhat uncertain regarding the merits of granting the gentleman's request.

A question sprouted in my mind: *Would Shelby, perhaps plagued by flashbacks of her abuse, recoil in fear, be reluctant or turn aggressive? What if he raised his arm to touch her, signaling to Shelby imminent violence or danger? What if she misread the stranger's intentions?*

The truth was I could not predict how she would interact with unfamiliar people. But I had to make a decision and I had to do it quickly.

"Sure," I responded to the elderly gentleman. Put on the spot, what alternative did I have? "We'd love to chat with you."

Feeling a rush of blood surge from my heart to my face, I hoped for a serene moment—nothing more, nothing less. Just let Shelby remain calm, even indifferent, I whispered.

Pausing, I knelt beside my faithful companion. "Shelby, see that man seated in the wheelchair?" I said, gesticulating in his direction with my right index finger, contradicting my sermonizing to my children that it was rude to point. "He wants to meet you. I'll take you over. He's elderly and ailing so we have to be gentle."

A moist nose nuzzled my hand, confirming she was willing. Approaching the gentleman, I instructed myself to breathe slowly and deeply. If I was calm, perhaps Shelby would pick up on it and, like a child, fall into imitation mode.

Just a few steps short of the wheelchair, Shelby's eyes met mine. I smiled. Rotating her head, she immediately fixed her gaze directly on the gentleman's face. I was no longer breathing.

When her tail began to flutter, my heartbeat intensified. I was incredulous. This was a perfect stranger. Usually shy and reticent with humans, Shelby needed time to sniff and study those who crossed her path. Even I had to exercise patience while cultivating a trusting relationship over time, before I was greeted with a tail wag!

Introducing Shelby to my parents and in-laws netted a timid reception. Making neither eye contact nor seeking proximity to another human, she presented herself as diffident and unavailable. Tucked low, the pit bull's tail remained immobile, her ears relaxed, limp in a sign of disinterest, and her sniff quotient totaled zero.

A sweet soul.

Shelby's was the typical demeanor of a mistrusting soul, fearful and uncomfortable in her surroundings, especially in the presence of those with whom she came into contact.

Prepared for a similar reaction, I stood mesmerized when the script in my head did not play out as expected. In fact, an interesting and totally unpredictable happenstance occurred.

Shelby scampered over to the gentleman, wagging her tail. Fascinated, I watched in silence, not daring to make a comment to Geralynn, who stood by, equally apprehensive.

"Hello, Shelby," the gentleman whispered, extending his arm to caress her. "You're such a sweet, beautiful dog."

Before I could bat an eyelash to clear my vision, Shelby placed her head firmly on the gentleman's knee. Taken aback by her atypical behavior, Geralynn and I exchanged questioning glances.

What just happened? Was I seeing correctly? Was this the hand of God? Is there a message here?

The gentleman's complexion brightened from the pasty hue of a shut-in shielded from the sunlight to an almost luminescent tone. Eyes, shrouded by the dimness of life's purpose lost, welled over with tears.

This scenario starred, in the role of protagonist, an utterly different Shelby. Though birds flew overhead, catching up on the day's events with their raucous chirping, and impatient drivers, anxious to get to the supper table, nervously tooted their horns, she stood her ground, neither losing focus with the distracting ruckus nor distancing herself. Instead, a kind, penetrating look and several licks along the twisted parameters of gnarled, arthritic fingers were the groundwork for a bond, linking the two.

It was amazing. Shelby found solidarity with a suffering man. Understanding his plight, she sympathized with his pain. Empathetic and patient, she offered assistance. Available, she graciously gave solace. Her shyness was invisible—her fear, non-existent. It seemed as if she never had a negative issue with another human being. But I knew better. Something beautiful and mystifying was at play here.

Captivated with Shelby, my attention wavered from the gentleman. Regaining my composure and concentration, I looked in his direction. Tears of joy rolled down his gaunt cheeks.

"Thank you, Shelby," he said, his voice quivering, "you made my day. You made me smile. I actually forgot about my pain—and all thanks to you."

What just happened? I questioned, flabbergasted.

I was reluctant to leave, as he continued to stroke Shelby's face. Several minutes later he reiterated his gratitude. Turning towards me, cordial and gracious, Shelby took several steps away from the gentleman, her mission fulfilled. After exchanging courteous pleasantries, we parted, bidding the gentleman a good evening.

In silence, we continued our walk.

"Geralynn, did you notice what happened?" I asked, ending the stillness.

"Yes, it was absolutely amazing—I couldn't believe my eyes. Joe, if I had not seen Shelby and the man firsthand, I'm sorry to say I may not have given credibility to this event."

Like a bolt of lightning searing through a cloud, an idea ran through my mind.

"Geralynn," I said, abruptly halting my steps. "That was astonishing. It was so inspiring. Did you notice how nurturing Shelby was—as if she understood his pain and need for compassion? She seemed to relate to him instantaneously—it was all so natural. Like two people who have just discovered a common bond! Nothing orchestrated, no training. I think Shelby could be a therapy dog! Maybe that is the meaning behind her own personal journey of suffering. Maybe that is why she was born and why she came to live with us."

Geralynn, still stunned by the unexpected, agreed. "That was awesome," she kept repeating over and over, perhaps trying to convince herself it actually occurred. "I would have never believed it. I think you are right—Shelby is a very special dog. If I adhered to theories of reincarnation, I'd say she was a philanthropic soul in the body of a pit bull!"

Chuckling, we continued walking. A gloaming dimness spread across the sky as the sun slipped into the horizon for a nightly rest. Though it was a relaxing setting, I could not break free of the thoughts churning and buzzing in my mind. I knew it was my mission to take action on the message the Lord sent me. Shelby's undertaking was to be a therapy dog. It was who she is. All she needed was certification.

I looked over at Shelby. He eyes were glowing. It was time to lower the curtain on the heavy manacles of a tortured yesterday and prepare for a new experience, fulfilling the Lord's plan unveiled this evening. Shelby received her wings, the manifestation of her purpose here on earth. I was not in error. There are canine angels.

The Evaluation

"They, too, are created by the same loving hand of God which created us... It is our duty to protect them and to promote their well-being."

—Mother Teresa

My thoughts following Shelby's extraordinary demonstration of nurturing and empathy became an ever-chanting mantra in my mind. Everything is part of a master plan; therefore, I knew I had to act on the sign I was given. The message was clear. But what exactly was my role in this scenario and how could I set it all in motion?

I had rescued and befriended the pit bull pup. In return, she had saved me from perhaps taking action when dire thoughts during a penetrating, all-consuming moment of depression scrambled my perspectives, placing me on the edge of an impending life-threatening cliff.

Undeniably, Shelby had given back. But now it was my turn to help her step into the role she was created to be. And I was neither willing nor able to deflect on this obligation.

"Joe, strolling downhill was easy, quick and fun, but now we have a pretty steep mound to climb," Geralynn said, interrupting my thoughts as we headed back to the car.

"Oh, it's not so bad," I responded unhesitatingly, grabbing her hand. "We'll take a deep breath and it won't be a problem. Don't forget we still have to burn off the yogurt calories."

Sharing a chuckle, we continued.

"Geralynn, nothing can ruin my mood. After Shelby's astonishing revelation, I'm on cloud nine. Do you understand the full impact of what she just demonstrated? Certainly there is an exciting following to be explored and developed and much to plan."

"Yes, it is wonderful, Joe, almost dream-like. I'm happy I was here to witness it."

But sometimes happiness is fleeting. Like a helium balloon let loose, it soon gets snatched in the wind's current, eventually becoming invisible to the human eye. Even trying to define happiness casts it in pause mode. Consequently, it is best left to enjoy, unquestioned.

Feeling a slight resistance on the leash, I gazed down at Shelby. Much as I would have fought any dark pressure aimed at smothering my joy, I could not deny she was struggling. Betrayed by her rhythmic panting, it was clear my pup was in agony as she limped along, trying to keep pace with us.

Following my lead, Geralynn's eyes focused on Shelby.

"Joe, I think Shelby's having a hard time."

Soft but laced with concern, her voice spoke words confirming the bitter truth. All the love and tenderness that Shelby extended could not eliminate the wounds so brutally inflicted.

Euphoria ricocheted into melancholy. I had to face reality—something very serious was wrong with Shelby's legs. No amount of love and kindness could override this reality. Denial, a convenient though worthless palliative, would only aggravate the issue.

Instead, I felt a pang in my heart. The delicate skin around my ears seemed on fire. I must have turned bright crimson. Concealed behind the last flicker of illumination in the early evening sky, a dark cloud waited in ambush. Shelby, on the other hand, a true heroine, seemed resigned to her crippling handicap, though it certainly came to her unbidden.

"I'll phone the vet in the morning and get an appointment to have her legs checked," I whispered to avoid alarming Shelby. Most dogs did not regard a trip to the vet with the same enthusiasm and upbeat spirit as a rendezvous for Frisbee at the beach, and the last thing on my mind was creating anxiety in my pup.

Decision made, I drove home, focusing on my next move with the same unwavering concentration I used in chess to checkmate my opponent's king.

Reaching the house, I parked and crossed over to open Geralynn's door. Quickly reversing my steps, I tugged the handle on the rear door and helped Shelby exit the car. When my 'ladies' were in the foyer, I darted to my computer, intentioned on Googling therapy dogs.

A professional dog trainer, I was familiar with Bright and Beautiful Therapy Dogs, Inc., a non-profit organization specializing in the evaluation, testing, training and certification of therapy pets. I liked their philosophy and goal to instruct 'charismatic' dogs with loving personalities, serene dispositions and compassionate hearts to act as angels of mercy, assisting the physically and emotionally challenged by bringing joy and camaraderie into their lives, adding long-lost smiles to grim faces.

Building on the concept of the dog in the role of man's best friend, Bright and Beautiful seeks to solidify this beautiful relationship for the benefit of mankind, from the elderly to toddlers, people with life-threatening illness, minor ills, learning disabilities, extreme loneliness and psychological issues, as well as chronic conditions and handicaps.

Therapy dogs also serve people facing dental or medical procedures, individuals plagued by emotional imbalances and those faced with bereavement due to the loss of a loved one.

In simple words, these four-pawed angels of mercy are faithful, loyal and empathetic best friends, always willing to *listen* with tolerant, accommodating ears, never rendering judgment or criticism. Responsive to the needs of others, they graciously interact, delivering affection in their own innocent way through licks, paw shakes and tail wags. Theirs is the hope to bring cheer. Theirs is the desire to distract mankind from the woes and obstacles sometimes pertinent to earthly existence.

Logging on to www.golden-dogs.org, the Bright and Beautiful website, the following day, I printed the list of qualifications and skills required to become certifiable as a therapy dog. Undoubtedly Shelby had the personality and compassion. *Did she fit the profile?*

I could hardly control my excitement. Tiny beads of sweat formed along my brow. With a brusque hand stroke, I wiped them away, never removing my gaze from the monitor. The moment was intense. *Could I flip this dream into a reality? Could I help Shelby obtain the necessary credentials to be a therapy dog? Was this truly her purpose?*

Of course, Shelby would need training—but that was the easy part. Though convinced of her intelligence, I was eager to test her aptitude for commands, an essential skill for service dogs

Easing myself out of the chair, I headed for the living room, where, at day's end, Shelby congregated with her canine siblings before retiring to their respective pens.

"Shelby, come with me outside for a moment," I said.

Immediately she slid off the sofa and stood beside me. Geralynn smiled.

"It's obvious she's in love with you," she said playfully.

"Is someone a bit jealous?" I teased. "Well, let's hope she loves and cherishes me enough to obey my commands," I chuckled. "If she cooperates, we can move forward on the training and certification."

Heading for the door, I slackened my steps to ensure Shelby a comfortable walk.

It was a delightful evening, balmy, though a hint of autumn was evident in the sprinkling of leaves on the freshly mowed lawn.

A bit more than a crescent moon greeted us. The glow reflected in Shelby's eyes; she took on an air of excitement even if her furrowed brow gave an inkling of bafflement. Unleashed, she was unsure of the nature of this outing.

"Shelby, I'm going to give you some commands. Please listen and follow my instructions," I said, petting her on the head.

Clearing my throat, I took a deep breath. My spirit invigorated with the anticipation of great achievement, I regarded Shelby's performance as the test of a lifetime. If she passed this, it meant she had the 'intelligence' to score high on the therapy dog exam.

"*Sit!*"

Immediately Shelby went down on her hindquarters. My pulse quickened. Trying to support the persistent effects of her injuries, she gently rocked back and forth. How willing she was to endure in lieu of disappointing me!

"*Come!*" Relieved, she stood, circled once then walked over to where I stood, leash in hand.

"Great, Shelby," I complimented.

When I slipped her head through the collar, she welcomed my hand with a lick.

I led her around the yard for a minute or two.

"*Heel!*" I blurted, unexpectedly, to catch her off-guard.

Shelby stopped short as if the brigadier general had given an order.

"*Down!*"

Instantaneously, she went on all fours. When I asked her to relax and get up, I cringed, noticing the hardship.

Leaning forward, I whispered, "Shelby, that was awesome—you're a natural."

Our eyes locked for an instant. Soon after, her tail wagged a 'thank you' for the compliment I had paid her. Gracious, she was.

Nothing could subdue my fervor—nothing could quash my drive to move ahead with Shelby's certification. All that skill demonstrated, in conjunction with her empathetic personality, pointed to a top-of-the-line therapy dog. However, the somber cloud passing the rainbow grounded my energy. *What if Shelby was too injured and unable to perform her duties? What if she was in too much pain?* I would never be a source of more agony in her life. That being the case, I would have to renounce my plans.

I observed Shelby intently for the next two days. Our appointment with the vet was scheduled at the end of the following week and I vowed to get her all the assistance needed to heal. In the meantime, I decided to move forward and see if Shelby could get more in-depth training and certification.

If it turned out her health would not permit the rigors of her new profession, I was resigned to let the idea go. Shelby's physical and emotional well-being were number one and took precedence over all else.

Although I was associated with a school that not only supplied trainers to instruct the dogs but set up the exam for certification, I opted to take the helm in hand and work with her personally. This would also give me the opportunity to observe her carefully to be certain she was neither in agony nor unfavorable to undertaking the program.

Ten days thereafter, I felt Shelby was well prepared. Proud of her accomplishments, I prayed her legs would not be the cause of undue misery until we had a chance to visit the vet and hear the diagnosis and prognosis. There had to be a cure. She was such a young pup.

Shelby's repertoire involved not only obeying basic commands and walking past a treat placed on the floor without retrieving it, unless permission was granted, but exercising tolerance for rough, clumsy or over-petting, as well as full body hugs that almost restrained breathing.

Moreover, she was adept at keeping her cool in front of confusion, elevated-volume voices/screaming and abrupt, staggering gesturing on the behalf of others. It was almost precision work to cover all the material she needed to master.

Asking Jenna and Joe to bang pots together, I trained her to demonstrate nonchalance in the face of ear-disturbing turbulence. But it did not end here. Since no aggressive reactions were allowed, Shelby had to gain savvy with wheelchairs, walkers and canes, people bumping into her (especially from behind), crowds, unruly children, other dogs and the exasperating impatience on the part of those she visited.

One thing was certain—Shelby lacked neither patience nor the enthusiasm to polish her skills. Despite her past trauma, she had little, if any, fear of human beings! It was absolutely amazing.

She was clever and motivated, and I felt the time was right. I'd take Shelby for the evaluation and if for some ill-fated circumstance her injury would be an insurmountable obstacle, nothing would come of it.

I set up the appointment for her evaluation on Sunday. Realizing she had not satisfied the requirement for a rabies injection, I scurried about until I located a vet clinic conveniently open on Saturday.

Shelby and I went over. As we waited in line, a gentleman and his two-year-old daughter exited the restroom station. The child spotted Shelby, scampered over and began playfully tugging at her ears, giggling incessantly. I held my breath! My pup stood statue-still. I realized this was another confirmation of her therapy dog aptitude and temperament.

Confident Shelby would earn a *cum laude* grade, I accompanied her to the testing station the following morning after mass. The evaluator, a kind, gracious man, greeted Shelby with a big smile and a warm head pat.

"Okay, let's get started. Shelby, *sit!*" he said, clearly and sharply, getting right down to business.

Standing by my side, Shelby remained motionless.

"Shelby, *come!*" Total paralysis! It was as if she was in another world! Commands she always obeyed to perfection during the

Shelby and me the day of her therapy dog test.

training sessions went unheeded. Today she seemed to be trapped in a catatonic stupor. *What could possibly be wrong? Something was disturbing Shelby—or was it just a crippling "SATs" anxiety?*

"Don't worry, Joe," the evaluator reassured, sensing my disappointment and frustration. "Take a fifteen-minute break and let Shelby calmly walk around." Apparently Shelby was picking up on her 'dad's' agitation.

Usually self-assured, she had no reason to doubt her skills; she was well prepared and had fully mastered the curriculum. I deduced it was a matter of test-day jitters.

Following the evaluator's advice, I took Shelby for a stroll.

Speaking to her softly, without any admonition, I reinforced her self-esteem.

"You can do this, Shelby," I whispered, leaning over to make eye contact. "We'll take a few minutes to unwind before giving it another try—and if it doesn't work out, it's no big deal. I still love you. I will always love you. You can never disappoint me—I know who you are!"

When she nuzzled my hand, my vision blurred. When her tail wagged, a tear ran down my cheek. A pair of sweet, contrite eyes looked apologetic.

"Okay, Shelby, let's give it another try!"

The evaluator was waiting. The stage was set. The ball was in Shelby's court. A short prayer accompanied by a pat on the head was the prelude to her second test.

I watched as Shelby obeyed every command with clean precision. Heaving a sigh of relief, I prayed she would complete part two of the test with equal bravura. Now came the more challenging 'issues.'

Giving Shelby a loving sidelong glance, I watched in silence as she passed the food test, fetching the treat and delivering it to the hand of the evaluator. The wheelchair, walker and cane exercises were also executed with utmost attention to detail.

When the clashing, clunking and screaming ruckus began, I held my breath. *How will Shelby react? Will she run scared, ears flat, tail tucked between her legs?*

I had my answer. Unruffled by the cacophony of multi-faceted noises, she ignored the pandemonium. She neither wavered nor panicked. Instead, her nonchalance was remarkable—she demonstrated a remarkable temperament for tolerance.

Next her interpersonal and inter-canine skills were tested. It was absolutely incredible. Shelby possessed the *savoir-faire* of a career diplomat. Swollen with pride, I was relaxed and enjoying my pup's performance.

The final test was a composure challenge. An unknown walked by and abruptly tweaked her ears. Poised like a debutante, Shelby stood motionless, completely unfazed.

"Great work, Shelby," the evaluator shouted, excited.

Hearing his commending words of praise, I ran over, smothering Shelby with kisses.

"Joe, you have one smart dog," he blurted, extending his hand in a congratulatory shake.

"Shelby, you are a therapy dog," he announced, gazing down at my tail-wagging pup.

Shelby knew she performed brilliantly. With her new empowering career, she also knew her family—human and canine—would be *head-swelling* proud. Shelby was right—as always!

I couldn't be more proud.

Onward to Wellness

"The time will come when men such as I will look upon the murder of animals as now they look upon the murder of man."

—Leonardo Da Vinci

M y joy advanced as my mind became increasingly excited with the notion of Shelby's new therapy dog career. There was, however, no comfort to my joy, as it was hauntingly embroiled in the melancholy and concern of her serious injuries.

Bittersweet, my excitement turned to anxiety as the day of Shelby's vet appointment neared. *What diagnosis would she receive and, more importantly, what prognosis would I have to accept?*

Regardless of the outcome, I would walk away grateful that Shelby had come into my life. I prayed, asking God to spare my little pup any further pain and agony, and I implored for the opportunity to do whatever humanly possible to help her heal or, at minimum, live her life under the best possible conditions.

If I could just take away the pathetic hobbling when on all fours and erase the look of anguish in her eyes, I would be *kneel-bending* grateful. Not limited exclusively to my prayer, the intention was also my promise to Shelby.

Anxiously I awaited the vet's visit. Though hopeful and intent on remedying the situation, my mind created diverse scenarios—unfortunately not all with positive outcomes. Mindful of the deleterious power of negative thinking, I made a conscious effort to dwell on and maintain an optimistic outlook.

However, observing Shelby closely, I could see the pain was worsening. Her movements were slowed, her stride deteriorating and when she tried to recline she would awkwardly drop on her stomach. Yet as much as she aspired to fit in with the antics and romping of Rommel, Greta and Spartacus, she was slipping. *How much more agony could this little pup handle?*

Dr. Louis Crupi awaited Shelby with all the sympathy of a serious, dedicated professional and animal lover. Turning a compassionate look upon her fearful face, he helped me lift her onto the visiting table.

"How are you Shelby?" he inquired in a calm, modulated tone. "Let's see if we can fix this problem." Sensing her apprehension and agitation Dr. Crupi gently caressed her head to induce relaxation before monitoring her heart with slow, studied motions.

Knowing my pup, I was aware of her restless state. Though a gentile man, Dr. Crupi represented a stranger, thus triggering in Shelby a certain dread of the unknown. I imagined she questioned, *Would he be a kind man like Dad and my brother Joe, or would he be brutal and abusive like those who inflicted my injuries?*

Timorous and retiring at first, perhaps reading my own mind, she eventually warmed to Dr. Crupi, sensing his righteousness in her regard. Finally I was able to breathe. Nevertheless, the degree and intensity of her wounds continued to chip away at my serenity.

Though excited about the possibilities of Shelby's new career, I vowed to forego any dreams if she was even minimally incapacitated or suffering pain. My priority was her well-being, and I was willing to undertake any hardship to achieve this goal.

A perfect patient, Shelby remained stoic, allowing Dr. Crupi free reign over her body. Meanwhile, I gave him a brief but poignant summary of her tortured life. Her enduring, almost imperturbable demeanor led me to believe she was either no longer experiencing pain or serene in the knowledge that the vet would make her whole again.

Did her unruffled comportment belie the truth?

"Dr. Crupi, it seems as if Shelby is not in any pain," I beamed, wanting to give credibility to my hurried judgment.

Attributing an errant status to my pain-free theory, Dr. Crupi resolved my dawning doubt.

"No, Joe. Sizing up the situation, I'd say this poor dog is in excruciating agony. The stoic demeanor is merely a testament to who Shelby is."

I knew he was right—in fact, I should have drawn my own conclusion.

"I'll need Shelby to remain here for some in-depth investigational work. But you can pick her up in the late afternoon. Don't worry, she'll be just fine."

Of course, I wasn't fretting her several hours at the vet's; I just feared any recurring thoughts of abandonment. I neither wanted her to feel abandoned again nor stir her past memory.

Returning to the house, I stewed over all the horrendous experiences my little pup had to endure in her short life. Uncertain of the actual nature of her experiences, my thoughts seesawed between the fantasy of Shelby telling me firsthand what had occurred and the wish to perhaps remain in the hypothetical realm. *How could I ever deal with the certainty of another human being savagely mistreating an innocent puppy?* Sometimes ignorance, if not actually bliss, can be somewhat reassuring, especially when it leaves room for the fabrication of convenient doubt.

After a careful evaluation, including palpation of the limbs, movement testing and x-rays, I returned to hear the diagnosis and bring Shelby home. Praying her condition was neither permanent nor life-threatening, I met with Dr Crupi.

"Joe, I'm afraid Shelby's injuries are rather complicated. Both knee joints in her hind legs need repairing." His voice was steady, earnest.

Though his conclusion came as no surprise, the confirmation of my fears stung nonetheless.

"I'm afraid Shelby will need extensive surgery to mend the damages. I can refer two reputable surgeons, one of which, Dr. Christopher Hunt, operates in the Animal Emergency and Referral Associates in Fairfield."

Since I was well acquainted with the pristine reputations of both Dr. Hunt and the clinic, I opted to take Shelby there. Immediately I called for an appointment. It was as if I were ablaze—on fire with a new, rejuvenating hope. Cognizant a plausible solution dangled on the horizon, I cared neither to flounder nor procrastinate.

The visit with Dr. Hunt was thorough and conclusive. Meticulously he reviewed Shelby's test results, blood work and radiographs along with Dr. Crupi's notes, written diagnosis and recommendations.

"Joe, can I ask you to walk around with Shelby? I'd like to observe her in motion."

Heeding his request, I walked several steps. Shelby followed suit, as always.

"I'll do some more testing and get back to you."

Following his own investigative work, Dr. Hunt phoned and I went to the clinic.

"Joe, I'm afraid Shelby has bilateral cranial cruciate ligament ruptures and a mild sciatic nerve deficit in the left stifle. Since CCL injuries are extremely common in dogs, I cannot confirm a diagnosis of abuse."

"She's such a young pup to be in this state," I said, shaking my head.

"Sometimes with repetitive activities, a progressive ligament degeneration and joint instability occurs, a condition leading to osteoarthritis. However, Shelby's sciatic nerve injury is unusual and probably related to an unknown traumatic injury."

"So something hurtful could have happened to her?"

"Perhaps—but I cannot know what that injury was."

Although Shelby's condition was not life-threatening, hearing about my sweet, young pup's surgical ordeal was like a noxious toxin invading my stomach, producing ripples of nausea. For a brief moment my clenched fists dug into the sides of my thighs. My balance faltered. Doubts remained in my mind regarding the nature of 'an unknown traumatic injury' in such a young dog and the pain it was causing her.

I tried to breathe, hoping to dislodge the weight burrowing down on my chest. Much as I struggled to calm the tsunami raging within, my efforts were powerless in the face of truth. In spite of Dr. Hunt's encouraging prognosis, nothing would or could ever free me from the unknowns in Shelby's life. I would forever question why she was abandoned, malnourished, injured and fastened to a tree in the garage station. It was devastating!

I needed a moment. It was one thing to have certainty and another to remain in the limbo of 'what really happened.'

As a result of my frequent visits to the shelter and from the endless conversations with Nancy and other staff members, I know that many animals are badly mistreated, even fatally abused, and then abandoned. Many face atrocious deaths, alone and in agony. It's shameful.

A compassionate man and professional, Dr. Hunt was visibly touched by Shelby's injuries. "Shelby needs surgery," he said, resting his gaze on my sweet, innocent pup. "The existing osteoarthritis indicates that the leg issues are not recent."

"Can you help her? Can you alleviate some of her pain?"

"Yes—the purpose of the surgery is to stabilize the joint, improve her strength and limit the development of future osteoarthritis. Actually this procedure carries a very good prognosis."

I started breathing again. Dr. Hunt's words were certainly reassuring. "What kind of surgery will you do?"

"I'll do a TPLO, tibial plateau leveling osteotomy, to repair the ruptured ligaments and give her an improved range of motion. I will work on the left stifle (leg) first as it seems in worse condition. Her quality of life will surely improve afterward."

Of course I gave my consent for the TPLO even after I was informed there was a $4,000-price tag per leg! There was no way I would deny my pup the help she needed—even if it meant working 24/7!

Hopefully Shelby's pain would soon be history. She had a loving, nurturing family and I would do whatever to restore her legs and health, thus guaranteeing the full life she deserved as a creature of God. Moreover, I knew in my heart that she had a very special purpose and I was determined to help her carry out her mission as an angel of mercy.

However, dreams apart, if there was even the slightest possibility that Shelby's condition would not permit her to be a therapy dog, it was no big deal. I knew she had what it takes to be one. Furthermore, she was a member of my family, cherished and accepted by all for her sweet, loving personality and for who she is.

Dr. Hunt set up the surgery, ran through the procedure as well as the pre-op and post-op protocol, and I took my pup home. Although I was encouraged by the prognosis, I was still overwhelmingly distraught over seeing my young pup in such a sad physical state.

A week later, on the day of the surgery, I prepared Shelby, speaking softly to her about the operation and how great she would feel once the convalescence and healing process was completed.

"Just a bit more distress," I reassured, "then you will be able to run and play like Rommel, Greta and Spartacus. But don't worry; Dr Hunt will do his best not to cause too much pain."

When her moist nose swept up and down along the back of my hand, I felt my eyes well over, much to my chagrin. I wanted to be strong for Shelby. Instead I was melting like a lighted candle caught in a delicate easterly breeze that refused to extinguish the flame as it quickly produced drippings of hot molten wax.

It was February 25, 2009, Ash Wednesday, a date I will never forget. The previous evening after drafting my *start of Lent* sermon, I had hardly closed my eyes, thinking about Shelby's surgical ordeal in the morning.

Restless, I twisted and turned, unable to drop off to sleep. Bouncing alongside me, willingly, or, more likely, unwillingly, Geralynn understood my state of mind.

"I'll drive you and Shelby to the hospital," she said as we finished breakfast.

"Will that interfere with your work schedule?" I asked. "If so, I could take Shelby myself. It's just a short ride."

"No, it will work out fine…besides, I'd really like to accompany you."

"Thanks, that will be great. I know Shelby would appreciate it," I murmured, no longer intent on concealing my desolation.

"Don't worry, everything will work out perfectly. I have a very good feeling."

"I hope so—I certainly invested a lot of prayer," I said, smiling perhaps for the first time in a week. Reaching over, Geralynn patted me on the shoulder.

"Have faith, Joe."

I was certainly not deprived in that category!

We drove to the Animal Emergency and Referral Associates, optimistic though fraught with the negative 'what ifs' that have a sinister way of creeping into the mind uninvited. Once there, the staff welcomed us with broad smiles, treating Shelby as a *VID*, very important dog, which everyone now knows she is.

Despite Dr. Hunts' extraordinary bedside manner and the comforting efficiency of his staff, the parting scene had all the elements of a true Aristotelian drama. I tried my best to summon all the self-control in my being, but when one of the assistant's reached out for Shelby's leash to accompany her to the OR, I took one last look at her innocent, melancholy face and dissolved in tears.

"It's Okay, Joe," the assistant whispered, "we'll take good care of Shelby. She's in excellent hands."

"Can I stay with her until the surgery? You know Shelby suffered being abandoned and abused. I want to reassure her as much as possible that she is in a loving setting."

Understanding my state of mind, and seeing my crimson, bloodshot eyes, she gave me a smiling nod, which gave me the green light. I needed nothing else.

In the waiting room, Shelby was relatively acquiescent, allowing the vet's assistant time to begin surgical preparation. I was told her leg would be shaved and she would be moderately sedated. Shortly thereafter a compassionate young woman took Shelby, giving me a sweet look, signaling it was time to leave. My heart raced.

Reassuring Shelby everything was going to be fine, I gave her two kisses, whispering in her ears that she would soon be back home with me, Geralynn and all her various siblings. As I distanced myself about a foot, my pup tried to lift herself up. Whimpering, she took several suffered steps in an attempt to follow me. Her eyes, filled with tears, met mine—an agonizing, lingering gaze.

"Joe, it's time to go," the assistant crooned in a barely audible tone. "Everything will be okay."

Turning, I blew Shelby a kiss and before crossing the threshold I looked over my shoulder at her standing there, following my every move. Suddenly my tears turned into convulsive crying. Geralynn came to my rescue, though her tear-stained cheeks were of little solace. Nevertheless, it was comforting to be in the company of someone who understood my misery. Although this was a healing, restorative surgical procedure in lieu of euthanasia due to a terminal illness, it hurt as much as the loss of a beloved pet.

Returning to my office, I pulled up my Ash Wednesday homily to add the finishing touches. Unable to concentrate, I stared at the silent phone. *Why doesn't it ring? Why no news from the hospital? Is Shelby okay? Is she out of surgery and in recovery? When can I take her home?*

It never dawned on me that perhaps I had more love, respect and concern for Shelby than, sadly, some parents demonstrate for their children. This is who I am and it reflects my belief in the sanctity and dignity of life in every species. All part of God's plan, He breaths life into His creatures for a specific reason. Therefore, man, animal, mammal, chordate (birds) and others deserve a fair chance to be who and all that they were born to be.

Before the distribution of ashes, I sat immobile in my office, eager to hear the piercing ring of my phone, not daring to absent myself even to use the restroom.

I prayed—long and hard. Before my conclusive *amen,* the phone rang.

"Good news, Joe," an enthusiastic voice shouted after my hello greeting. "Shelby is out of surgery. The procedure was complicated but went well. She will..."

"Can I come now to get her?" I blurted, truncating his sentence.

"No, Joe, I'm sorry. Shelby has to remain overnight for observation and medication. But she is resting comfortably."

Somewhat reassured, I headed over to church.

Noticing my puffed, ruby-red eyes, some parishioners approached.

"Deacon Joe—is everything all right? Is something wrong?"

"No, no, everything is okay." I fibbed a bit even if it was Ash Wednesday and the start of the Lenten season. Truly, it was the lesser of two evils because if I told the story, I'd end up wailing like an infant in the throes of a colic attack.

Eager for the day to end so I could bring my pup home, I retired

Shelby, content at home.

early. As luck would have it, I was the victim of anxiety insomnia, which ironically elongated the anticipation. Minutes ticked away like hours—hours seemed to melt into days. Finally a flicker of light sent a shadow across my wall. Dawn, gracious and promising, had broken the agonizing spell.

I rose, showered and dressed—in silence.

A call to confirm Shelby's discharge frazzled my already fragile nerves.

"Joe, Shelby will be ready after twelve!"

Agonizing through a business lunch, I tired to be nonchalant about checking the time every ten or fifteen minutes. However, lifting my right arm periodically to view the face of my timepiece did not accelerate the passage of hours.

Returning home, I freshened up before heading over to the hospital.

"I'm off to bring Shelby home," I announced to Geralynn, Joe, Jenna and the other dogs. "She's coming home!" I enjoyed their collective enthusiasm.

Smiling, I drove to the hospital. When I arrived, I was asked to wait.

"Shelby will be out in a minute. Dr. Hunt is checking her before the release."

I sat. The moment the door creaked open, I jumped to my feet. The nice woman who had attended her earlier stood in the doorway. I inched closer. Slowly, she led Shelby through the door. Weak and unsteady on her feet, my pup looked pathetically despondent.

"Hello, Shelby. How nice to see you. I missed you. We all missed you," I blurted.

A melancholy, unfocused gaze gave her a lost feeling. It was heartbreaking. Looking her over with my eyes, I noticed her tail was motionless, frozen between her legs. The horrendous memory of my first meeting with Shelby in the shelter flashed through my mind. This pup did not seem like Shelby Dwyer. This despondent dog was the abused pit bull cowering in the rear of her pen in the shelter!

The lump in my throat thickened. I felt as if I would choke to death. *Did Shelby relive her feelings of neglect and torture? Did she think I abandoned her? Did she think she would never see me again? Was her faith in me irretrievably shattered?*

"Hello, Shelby," I said, darting to her side. Dropping on my knees, I gave her a gentle, loving caress. It would destroy me if, in fact, she felt betrayed. *But how would I convince her otherwise?*

Suddenly a warm, dry tongue brushed against my hand. I covered her face with kisses as a swishing echo signaled her tail was wagging against the bandages. My pup knew I would never abandon her. Thrilled to see me, she knew she was going home.

"*Thank you, God,*" I whispered, realizing Shelby was on the first lap of a long journey toward a full recovery.

Obstacles
Along the Path

"Animals, as part of God's creation, have rights which must be respected. It behooves us always to be sensitive to their needs and to the reality of their pain."
—Dr. Donald Coogan, former archbishop of Canterbury

Now that Shelby's first surgery could be referred to in the past tense, I found myself suddenly cast in the role of primary caregiver. Though I exercised my new 'profession' with love, dedication and an unwavering commitment to render this period comfortable and serene to promote a fast and complete recovery, I realized managing the post-op convalescence of an energetic pup would be a rather challenging task.

"Joe, Shelby's recovery is a four-month rehabilitation process," Dr. Hunt said upon discharging her. "You must listen carefully and follow every instruction with utmost precision. Your diligence will determine the speed and nature of her recovery."

I had to commend Dr. Hunt for his excellent instructions. Easy to follow, they made my life less complicated, especially once I got organized and more familiar with the different steps.

There was a precise medication schedule, meticulous wound

care and appropriate exercise at gradual levels of increased intensity to ward off skin suffocation and the resulting painful bedsores.
Furthermore, precautions were needed to avoid serious, even life-
threatening, infections due to less-than-scrupulous attention to
prohibit a bacteria-infested environment.

Additionally, the dangers of dehydration and renal failure
from diarrhea, vomiting and an insufficient consumption of fluids
were a real threat. And to promote healing, I had to wear the hat
of a nutritionist/chef, preparing and serving well-balanced meals
in conjunction with the appropriate administration of vitamins
and minerals.

However committed, my spirit rebelled against shadowy
thoughts; any inklings of failing at this very special mission were
dismissed at the onset. Shelby would do just fine. Soon she would
be running on all fours. In my mind was a budding awareness that
sometimes the mysterious unknown buffers anxiety even if for just
a fleeting moment in time. Still, intentions are an influential force
and, intermingled with prayer, they take on an empowering role.

Dr. Hunt had fitted Shelby with a cumbersome Elizabethan
collar, a cone-shaped lampshade contraption designed to prevent
her from gnawing, scratching or licking her wounds. Though a
necessary healing aid, it looked terribly uncomfortable as it greatly
constrained her head movements. Seeing her so constricted saddened me.

Badly engorged from the surgical trauma, her leg had to be
intermittently iced to reduce swelling, thus decreasing some of the
pain and stiffness from the incision and the actual procedure.

Despite my angst and her perturbing distress, my philosophi-
cal pup tried to make the best of a trying experience. A model
patient, she allowed me to fuss over her even if my touch was
perhaps not as graceful as Dr. Hunt's. Presumably her intuition
told her my interventions, though lacking professional savvy, were
filled with love.

The rehabilitation of her knee was certainly not without

anguish. However, whimpering and often trembling in pain, she eyed me with a trusting, all-permissive gaze that tugged at my heartstrings. Conscious of her excruciating ordeal, I also realized the merit she would gain from endurance.

Nevertheless, understanding my unfaltering love and devoted commitment to her every need and wish, she licked my hand from time to time in an expression of gratitude for collaborating on her rehab mission.

Most of the therapeutic regimen I had mastered within the first week. Somehow it all fused together in an almost ideal manner, until the passage of time created havoc with the exercise routine.

She was a young, energetic pup and it became a Herculean task to restrict her movements to short, moderate-pace walks when she would rather unself-consciously try to push forward at a faster stride. Of course, on the positive side, her insistence on speed acceleration in lieu of a placating, sedentary lifestyle signaled the pain was diminishing and the leg was healing.

When Shelby started kicking up little clouds of dust, I knew she was out of the woods at least with respect to the right leg. Now my poor pup faced additional surgery to repair her left limb. This meant an encore of the previous four-month recovery period.

Meanwhile, the summer solstice had arrived, ushering in longer days and steamy, hot temperatures. Looking at Shelby reclining under a huge oak tree, I wondered if I could perhaps postpone the second surgery until autumn winds sent the crisp, coiled leaves twirling along the surface of my backyard. With cooler weather I was certain the surgery would be easier to endure, which, in turn, would quicken healing. My mind set on a seasonal postponement, I phoned Dr. Hunt in the morning.

"Doctor, I'd like to move Shelby's surgery to a later date," I said. "Do you think this would create a problem? Because of her high energy, with the onset of warmer days, she's starting to enjoy the outdoors, romping with the other dogs, and I think it will give her a break after all she has suffered during the past few months.

Furthermore, the postponement will allow me some quiet time to recharge before starting the process all over again. Could we perhaps consider late fall?"

Unfortunately, my persuasive skills were not very savvy that day—though I was able to negotiate a couple of months' flexibility for Shelby.

"Joe, a few weeks will not make that much of a difference, but do not let it go too far past the summer. Let's schedule it for September."

Although Dr. Hunt probably did not accept my reasoning with conviction, he did concede some breathing time, which I was certain Shelby needed and would enjoy after the ordeal. Grateful, I expressed my appreciation for the time off and set the second surgical procedure.

My ultimate goal was for complete healing and a closed-door policy on Shelby's abuse and resulting consequences. My wish for her was physical and emotional wellness, a pain-free existence and the energy to move on to the next very important part of her life— nurturing and inspiring other victims of suffering and adversity.

Browsing through my favorite scriptural passages and prayers one afternoon, I came across a quote authored by St. Francis of Assisi, a deacon and preacher who was known and revered as the patron saint of animals. I always felt a certain affinity for this kind and pious friar, especially on his feast day, October 4, when many churches conduct a special service to bless the animals of the parish. Of course, I look forward with joy and enthusiasm to conducting this blessing in my own church.

Thinking of Shelby, I repeated his words; *"Not to hurt our humble brethren is our first duty to them, but to stop there is not enough. We have a higher mission—to be of service to them when-ever they require it."*

I could not be more in agreement and had vowed early on to be of service to Shelby, especially during her recovery.

July and August sped by with supersonic speed. Shelby was

gaining strength and dexterity in her right leg, though her pain-ridden left limb kept her unbalanced and limping. Dr. Hunt was right to discourage me from waiting. In the end it would only hurt my pup. Her ligaments were ruptured and had to be repaired—the sooner, the better.

Unconsumed with exaggerated worry, I slept pretty well the night before Shelby's second surgery. The following morning I watched as she stretched, took a few sloppy licks of water and walked over to my side for the morning ritual with Rommel, Greta and Spartacus.

Focusing my attention on her, I caressed her head.

"Shelby, Dr. Hunt is waiting for us. He is going to operate and fix your right leg. Everything will be just fine." Since Shelby was more than adept at picking up on my moods, I tried my best to speak in a reassuring tone.

Geralynn came over, reinforcing my words.

"Everything's going to be just fine, Shelby," she whispered, giving her a kiss.

After Geralynn and Shelby exchanged emotional goodbyes, I slipped on her leash and escorted her to the car.

I drove to the hospital that last day of September, somewhat less apprehensive, though for added security I prayed. There was certainly no harm in asking God for help. Subsequently, my thoughts slipped into the pernicious *what if* scenarios in a *déjà vu* scene, previously enacted. Breaking the spell cast on me as the victim of some gloomy witchcraft, I repeated with ferocious persistence, *"Don't worry. Everything is just fine. Everything is just fine. Everything went well the first time. Everything will be fine this time. It's going to be okay."*

My mind was yearning—burning for the same positive outcome. Nevertheless, it was Shelby's serene attitude that calmed my spirit. If she had faith—if she was all-trusting—who was I to wallow in sudden doubt?

The procedure was basically the same. Shelby was shaved,

sedated and brought into the ER. Once again her melancholy gaze, fixed on mine during the parting, disrupted my composure. Although I had withstood all that destiny had imposed, I had to admit my self-control took on the callous maliciousness of a traitor, leaving me sobbing in the waiting room.

My pup was dually a joy to my heart and a cause of misery due to her forlorn past and ensuing physical impediments. She touched my heart in ways I would have never dreamed imaginable. Maybe it was her pain. Maybe it was her innocence. Maybe it was her vulnerability. Maybe it was her sweetness in the face of such cruelty demonstrated in her regard. Or maybe it was her extraordinary ability to love, nurture and forgive mankind for those who truly *trespassed against her.* As time passed, I understood that neither rancor nor vengeance was part of her makeup!

En route to my office, I obliged my thoughts to turn positive. By day's end, I would receive word of another Dr. Hunt success. Then it was up to me to carry out my Florence Nightingale pledge, to nurse my special pup back to health and vigor. I would not quit until Shelby was on all fours running around the yard like a two-year-old pup.

Surprisingly, Dr. Hunt's call arrived mid-morning, curtailing the furtherance of nervous fretting.

"Joe, great news—the surgery went well. Shelby did wonderfully. We will keep her here for medicating and monitoring overnight and you can come get her in the morning."

"Thanks, Dr. Hunt—thanks for taking care of Shelby," I blurted, relieved to hear the good news.

"Well, she's a model patient," he responded. "Now, it's up to you to nurse her back to a full recovery over the next four months."

"No problem. I will do all in my power to hasten her healing."

Reassured, I whispered a prayer of appreciation and gratitude before returning home to reorganize my do-it-yourself 'nursing station.'

Too excited to sleep, I arose the following morning before dawn signaled the start of a new day.

"It's still dark—where are you going?" Geralynn whispered, her eyes still shut from the evening's rest abruptly cut short.

"I can't sleep. Maybe I'll get ready to pick up Shelby."

"But you have plenty of time—why not relax and get some more rest?"

I gazed over at her with a suffered, impatient look.

"Okay, Joe—go get ready!"

I had to be thankful for the wonderful marriage Geralynn and I shared. Undoubtedly, she understood my psyche—even my silent communications.

Hurriedly, I showered and dressed, forgoing my fitness routine. The aroma of fresh-brewed coffee confirmed my blessings. While I showered, Geralynn had headed to the kitchen to prepare some breakfast.

"Thanks, Geralynn," I muttered, feeling a bit guilty about getting her up at such an ungodly hour. Yet despite my impatience, she had a certain fluid calmness that complemented my own emotional impulsivity.

Picking up Shelby was an encore presentation of the previous post-surgery event. But this time, in spite of the of the coercive Elizabethan collar inhibiting head movement, she quickened her pace as soon as she spotted me seated in the waiting room. There was another of our very special moments of private bonding, then I was handed my instructions and invited to phone the hospital in the event a problem would arise.

No longer a novice, I felt confident I could breeze through the next four months with few, if any, impediments. Aware of the protocol, I drove home certain our troubles were just remembrances to be eventually deleted from our minds. I cared not to have Shelby settle into a role wherein she would forever remain a detainee of her dreadful past. Instead, I wanted the bliss of a full recovery—with no tattered threads dangling as a souvenir of her excursion through hell.

Nonetheless, I soon discovered that certainty is but a component of perhaps the after-life. Nothing and no one should ever be taken for granted. Around the corner lurks the unforeseen—floundering possibilities and bewildering conjecturers that contradict all that we sometimes believe to be a secure reality.

Two weeks into her convalescence, I noticed Shelby began excessively favoring her left leg, refusing to evenly distribute her weight on both limbs, which she had been doing during the initial days of the post-surgical period.

Concerned, I phoned Dr. Hunt, who advised me to bring her in for a check-up. After a careful examination of the wound, he diagnosed an infection at the incision site. I cringed, imagining the resulting pain.

"Joe, I'm going to prescribe some antibiotics to clear up the infection. Shelby will have to remain on the medication for at least the next two months. At the end of that period, once the antibiotics are suspended, I will re-evaluate the situation. If the infection is cured—we're in luck! However, if it persists, it may mean the screws and plates will have to be removed and replaced."

I was devastated. Everything was going so smoothly until now. What could have possibly gone wrong? My faith in Dr. Hunt's surgical capabilities was unwavering; therefore, I vowed to maintain a positive outlook. Additionally, I didn't want to discourage Shelby with any doom-and-gloom attitude. *We have come this far—we will not only prevail, but conquer,* I said to myself. Nothing would interfere with Shelby's journey toward wellness. She was a survivor, and I felt secure she would overcome even this hurdle.

I prayed for added security and the Lord responded. *Was it in gratitude for my loyalty and faith in His mercy? Or did He also develop a special feeling for Shelby?*

Two months thereafter, upon finishing her course of antibiotic treatment, I brought Shelby in for a check-up. Although I could tell

Recovered from surgery, Shelby played in the snow with Spartacus.

from her graceful walk she was no longer in excruciating pain, I would not breathe easy until Dr. Hunt gave me the *all-clear* verdict on her infection.

Shelby stood beside me, wagging her tail with wide, sweeping motions. No one could ever persuade me into thinking she did not recognize Dr. Hunt's merits. Convinced of her intelligence and almost psychic, precise intuition, I was certain my pup knew he had played a major role in fixing her legs. With broad rhythmic tail swoops and glistening eyes, she conveyed her thanks.

Soon she was romping and jumping with Rommel, Greta and Spartacus. Like a healthy, energetic pup, making up for lost time, she ran swiftly, overtaking her canine siblings with her long, muscular legs. She was pain-free; all that remained were the huge scars, occupying three-quarters of the inner surface of her hind legs—an indelible reminder of Shelby's personal crucifixion and an enduring testament to her forbearance, tenacity in the face of adversity, strength of character, determination to overcome and sweet, loving personality. The power of love and prayer—indisputable.

Undoubtedly, Shelby is a very special pup. But I already knew that from day one at the shelter, even before I received confirmation *via* eyewitness evidence.

Shelby's strength of character has enabled her to overcome all obstacles.

From Abused
and Abandoned
to Celebrity Status

*"But ask the animals and they will teach you...which of these
does not know that the Hand of God has done this."*
—Book of Job 12:7-9

Dark clouds no longer loomed overhead like menacing vultures, trying to bully the advent of a promising winter season soon to bud. In fact, nothing could intrude on the serenity I felt after the tempest of the past eight months had settled into just a bad memory.

Healed, rehabilitated and in the prime of her life, Shelby was eager and ready to be who she was born to be—a therapy dog. And delegated as her emissary, I was intent on doing all in my power to help her achieve full potential.

Realizing I would not be able to sleep until I had a precise strategy, I decided to take some time to devise a plan that involved researching and locating a facility that would be willing to accept Shelby on a flexible timetable, since my own schedule as vice chancellor was hectic and somewhat erratic. Consequently, I knew it would be difficult to commit to the organized weekly itinerary most facilities required.

When I contacted Bright and Beautiful, where Shelby had been evaluated, tested and certified, I received e-mails in response from diverse facilities outlining an almost regimental schedule, impossible for me to adhere to. However, like the father of a bright child just graduated from college, I was eager to see my pup in action, applying her talents for the benefit of others.

Though I cared not to be presumptuous, I knew my Shelby was gifted and blessed with special talents. Undoubtedly, she was born with a glowing pair of wings. Soon they would be visible for all to see. Whenever I gazed at her I felt a swelling pride as if I were seated in the audience while she delivered an eloquent 'thank you' tribute after winning the Nobel Peace Prize.

But I wasn't alone in my adulation for the abused pit bull pup. Anyone who had met Shelby was completely sucked in by her warm, sweet personality and gentle, endearing charm. It was easy to bond with such a gracious dog.

Extroverted despite the abuse, her open manner gave me the impression I had truly shared one of the most poignant experiences of her short life. For this reason our relationship was indeed precious. There are those who fully understand this magical connection and there are those who for many reasons cannot. Perhaps it's the same chemical reaction that draws people together and pulls others apart.

Now that she was pain-free, Shelby trotted like a thoroughbred filly, rhythmically swinging her *derrière,* thrilled with her own quick stride. Both incredulous and thankful for medical miracles, I sat following her every move with insatiable eyes. Meanwhile she gazed at me quizzically. Relaxing my glance, I questioned over and over, as if repetition would guarantee a response: *Did Shelby know I was hard at work trying to find a facility she could serve? Was she aware of the comforting power given to her?*

Her bark, in sync with the shrill echo of the telephone ring tone, shattered my incantation.

"Hello, Mr. Dwyer?" a strong voiced resonated.

"Yes, speaking. How may I help you?" I queried in response.

"Mr. Dwyer, I'm calling on behalf of the Easter Seals Facility for people with developmental disabilities to follow up on an e-mail sent earlier regarding our decision to welcome your dog Shelby to our rotating therapy dog staff. Can you take her in for some orientation tomorrow?"

Did I hear correctly?Did Easter Seals just welcome Shelby to their therapy dog staff?

Hands trembling, I returned the receiver to the cradle. My heart pounded to a new and different beat. Unable to catch my breath, I feared I would go into arrhythmia and collapse.

The Easter Seals Facility, catering to adults of various ages with development disabilities, is an amazing non-profit organization which had opened its doors for more than half a century to individuals with special needs—autism, physical handicaps, genetic or acquired, and psychological issues. Their mission *"to help people and families with disabilities and special needs to live, work, and play in their communities with equality, dignity, and independence,"* was in keeping with my own ministry of service to others.

Knowing that Shelby would be a part of this amazing organization was exhilarating. I had to tell Geralynn and the kids; they would be so proud of Shelby, especially after she had fought so nobly and defeated her demons with an impressive display of courage. Rising from the chair, I noticed my knees shook from excitement.

"Shelby!" I shouted. "Easter Seals has asked for your service! Isn't that phenomenal?"

For a brief interval, stillness prevailed, just before her tail swished back and forth in wide, sweeping motions, like the steady hand of an animated flamenco dancer fluttering her fan to create a cooling breeze. I feared it would somehow break loose from the rapid movement.

No one could have ever convinced me Shelby didn't know her new career was about to take off. I hugged her as we shared a special moment of triumph, a moment in which a settling of the score for all the pain and suffering endured had begun to take form. Shelby, of course, was anything but vindictive. Hers was a philosophy of surrender—letting go and moving on.

Several mornings later, waiting for the coffee to brew, I gazed over at the calendar Geralynn had placed beside the telephone to prohibit life's distractions from causing slip-ups with important events and appointments. Some of us are sometimes a bit forgetful—or as we say, consumed by life's bustling nature.

I noted it was June 5, 2009. I also noted this date would be remembered as the day my pup stepped into who she is. Nothing could ever compare to my joy this day—to the gratification of having fought a bloody battle—to the exhilaration of having risen from the trenches, bloodied and wounded, to stand triumphant, undefeated despite the barrage of curveballs maliciously pitched. Shelby did.

Day by day the changing expression in Shelby's eyes brought hope. Would she ever forget those who had assailed her? The scars were deeply etched on her inner thighs—souvenirs of suffering and valor. I prayed her recollection would fade. I prayed she would one day no longer know the details of her early life. I prayed for lost memories.

"Joe, I think the coffee is burning," Geralynn shouted from the bedroom.

"I have it under control" I lied, mopping up the spill after I poured too fast.

"Don't step here, Shelby," I whispered, "you'll burn your paws with the hot coffee."

I could be wrong—or maybe not—but I was certain my pup was laughing.

Alone with her thoughts, there was no doubting her mind was filled with a true understanding of what was happening. I leaned over, finished removing the evidence of my distraction and planted a kiss on the head of my accomplice. In return I received a sticky lick. Now I was certain—she got it!

Anxiously I gulped down breakfast, thankfully escaping choking to death. Shelby, meanwhile, stood by quietly observing. Afterward I returned to my bedroom, pulled open the drawer and picked up the red bandana and TDI tag that comprised the therapy dog uniform. Tying it around her neck was a bit challenging as she insisted on playfully licking my hand. But once in her regalia, Shelby assumed the pose of a Marine, proud to wear a symbol of honor and merit.

Off we went to the Easter Seals Facility in Rochelle Park, New Jersey. The drive was short. Lost in our thoughts, we traveled in silence. Fifteen minutes thereafter, Shelby and I crossed the threshold into the facility.

Respectfully, with head lowered, Shelby remained by my side as I made the introductions. A young man bent down to check Shelby's TDI tag.

"Hi, Shelby," he said, reading her name from the ID. "We're so happy to have you with us today."

I looked around and noticed the demographics at the day care center included adults from age twenty to around the mid-to-late fifties. Many were physically challenged; others, psychologically and/or intellectually. All seemed excited to see Shelby.

Within minutes of her entrance, a group had formed around her. Hands reached out to pet her, arms tried to encircle her body in big, sometimes clumsy bear hugs while I held my breath, wondering how Shelby would handle her first day on the job.

At ease despite the sudden rush to grab her, she slowly lowered herself to the floor, allowing more people easier access. At first I mistook her gesture for nervousness or fear, but seconds later learned it was the result of a clever mind at work to devise a functional strategy.

One man cradled Shelby's head in his large, calloused hands.

A woman went down on her knees, grabbing her middle, while a young, slender girl rubbed her face across my pup's lower back. All were smiling and relaxed. All were enveloped in the moment—their disabilities and failings, anxieties and sadness neither a definition of who they are nor a priority in their lives.

When a giggling young boy walked over and gently tried to catch her wagging tail, I lost it. Rotating my head away from the moving scenario, I tried to conceal my own emotional release. It was absolutely amazing to see frowns, melancholy gazes and bent shoulders supporting lowered heads suddenly melt into smiles, chuckles and lifted heads.

In reality, nothing had changed—the afflicted with Asperger's Syndrome or autism were not suddenly socially interactive or verbally communicative, and people with developmental disabilities were not unexpectedly healed, but somehow the presence of one pit bull pup had enabled those with problems to momentarily postpone their issues. Plagued by varying degrees of developmental failings, many residents could neither conceptualize nor control their own physical strength. Consequently, more often than not, Shelby had to bear the discomfort of heavy-handed caresses and less-than-gentle squeezes and hugs.

However, it mattered not to Shelby. Unflinching and practically immobile except for her fluttering tail betraying a bit of emotion, she remained somewhat stoic, though openly available to all. Understanding the plight of others, she knew the reason for her visit was to nurture those in pain. This was not about Shelby. It was about her mission as a canine angel.

Many who were usually silent tried to speak to Shelby, repeating her name over and over.

"Shelby, you are so pretty—you're a darling." Both residents and staff were enamored. Undeniably, it was love at first sight. I felt a mysterious stirring of energy in the room, an unexplainable, calming force.

To see the joy and fulfillment flourish in those impeded by varying degrees of limitations who gathered around her like swarms of yellow-jacket bees searching for a source of energizing nectar was an incredible experience. It elevated me up into the clouds, momentarily eradicating my own dark dealings with depression and anxiety.

Charismatic, sweet and loving, Shelby was an immediate success. Perhaps her own torturous experiences of abuse, neglect and, I'm certain, at times unbearable pain contributed to the development of the empathetic and tolerant side of her temperament.

At one point four individuals approached, smothering her with kisses. There were no boundaries—her entire body was unbolted territory for love and affection. And with the patience of a saint, she endured the love-fest.

Towards the end of the visit, a large, multi-colored sheet cake was wheeled out in celebration of one of the resident's birthday. Serenaded with an off-key 'happy birthday' melody and applauded, he was then offered the first slice. Shortly thereafter, a scrambling of feet stampeded toward the table, with the same drive of twenty thoroughbreds sprinting the moment the stall gates fly open. A mingling of hands from frail and slender, massive and gnarled, to stiff and limited grasped for a much yearned for treat.

I stood a spectator on the sidelines, not particularly desirous of getting entangled in the sudden onrush. Within minutes, the originally spotless floor was turned into a mosaic of crumbs and trampled icing remnants. Bewildered by the chaotic scenario, I continued to nurse my beverage between the palms of my hands, gently rotating the cup back and forth with the same movements I used to wind my first watch as a young lad.

The staff was phenomenal—indulgent, patient and caring.

"Is she your only dog?" a young female attendant asked.

"No, I have three others, but Shelby's the only one with the therapy dog vocation."

"Did you have her a long time? You seem very close."

"Actually, not that long. I rescued her from a shelter less than a year ago," I responded, beaming.

"Do you know her story?" another staff member chimed in. "Who would give up such a beautiful and fabulous dog?"

When I related the vicissitudes of her tragic beginning, moist eyes responded to the horror tales of abuse and suffering as well as her inspiring journey back to wellness.

"We can see why she is so special."

Others were beginning to understand what I knew from day one. Shelby was no ordinary pit bull pup. In my mind she was the canine version of the biblical Job. In suffering, there is merit and those called to endure pain are given a special strength to endure and overcome. Much was given to Shelby.

Once the attendants had excused themselves from my company, my gaze caught Shelby's. However much as I tried to hold it, the distractions were just too overpowering. Turning her head from side to side, she seemed mesmerized by the new surroundings and eager to decipher exactly what was happening.

Most dogs would not be able to remain unperturbed in the face of a floor covered with such a delectable treat. *What would Shelby do? Would she weaken and fall prey to temptation? Would she lower her head and snatch a crumb or two, believing no one was looking? And if she did weaken, who would notice? Would it really matter? Or would she continue to be impassive, as she was trained?*

As quickly as I posed the questions, the answers arrived. Shelby did absolutely nothing. Fighting temptation, she kept her head lifted, not yielding even to a few perhaps illicit sniffs.

Amazingly she had carried out her first mission visit with the savvy, self-confidence and diplomatic *savoir-faire* of an experienced career-therapy dog. Nothing ruffled her feathers—neither the audible bedlam of laughter and voices nor the personal jostling and nudging of heavy-handed individuals—not the impact with the unfamiliar nor the suddenly-turned-edible floor.

Lying around the house in good spirits.

On the way home, I repeated over and over in my mind, *What an amazing dog Shelby is.* Looking over my shoulder at a red light stop, I noticed she was totally prostrate, drained of all her forces. However, despite the sheer exhaustion of having given so generously of her energy, the serenity on her face spoke of personal satisfaction. Shelby knew she had been a healer.

While she slept, I thought of the parable recounted in Chapter 8: 44-45 of St. Luke's Gospel, in which a woman who had suffered from incurable hemorrhaging for twelve years had *"come up behind Jesus, touched the tassel of His cloak and at once her hemorrhage ceased."*

When Jesus' question regarding who had touched Him met with firm denials, He responded, *"Someone touched me for I perceived that power had gone forth from me."*

Likewise it was with Shelby—her power had just gone forth from her.

Feeling almost foolish for the nervous energy I wasted on the ever-ridiculous 'what ifs' of negative thinking, I scolded myself for not knowing better. Of course Shelby would not fail. She knew exactly who she was, where she was, why she was there and what she was supposed to do. And she did—she did it all with utmost grace and perfection, with unwavering love, caring and nurturing.

On her maiden visit to the Easter Seals Facility, I had received confirmation of what I always suspected. My Shelby is incredible. I was so proud of her. Undeniably, she was on a special journey.

The True Meaning of Forgiveness

"For the lot of man and of beast is one lot... Both have the same life-breath and man has no advantage over beast... Both go to the same place... Both were made from dust and to dust they both return."

—Ecclesiastes 3: 19-20

Although I surely neither needed nor required validation of my belief that animal life is to be respected and cherished just as human existence, reading Ecclesiastes 3, verse 19-20 confirmed the common fate shared between the species. In the end we all reach the final destination of our journey physically, just a heap of dust either cast into oblivion for a selfish, squandered life, criticized for wicked ways and evil intent toward others, or revered and admired for having truly contributed to the betterment of earthly creatures.

Of course, any advocate of the Divine Creation theory has an obligation to regard all living organisms as gifts from God. Therefore, my feelings toward Shelby from day one centered on an utmost compassion for her sorry lot, love for her sweet innocence and respect for her right to a dignified life.

Consequently, with every visit to the Easter Seals Facility, I shared in Shelby's joy and gratification while witnessing contorted, melancholy and wasted faces relax and break into genuine smiles in her presence. Observing the stumbling blocks of serenity—unwanted silence and anxiety, pain and frustration—no longer obstruct happiness, I reflected on the power Shelby held in her paws and empathetic gaze.

To know moments of contentment, to be liberated from the failings of the human condition, to actually consummate life as it was meant to be were my pup's offerings, though she knew not the value of her precious gifts to others.

During Shelby's troubled times, when she was dealing with neglect and maltreatment coupled with the after-effects of the trauma, she had utilized the experience to regenerate her innate resources of nurturing and compassion. The sheer monstrousness of her early months gave her a special power. Thus it was my intention to develop and broaden her therapy dog career path.

However, most of the e-mail requests I received from Bright and Beautiful were based on a set schedule, which I was unable to satisfy due to my own professional obligations. Meanwhile, undaunted by temporary setbacks, my enthusiasm continued to grow, bubbling over like chilled Champagne poured all too rapidly into tall, angular flutes.

Whenever I looked at Shelby, I noticed an almost begging willingness in her eyes. Bright and expressive, they had a special way of communicating the thoughts and yearning locked within her heart. A slightly askance head, a pair of asymmetrically erect ears and an unpredictable, restless stirring when at rest told me she needed to assist others—summoned me to make it happen.

The message was clear-cut. I couldn't ignore her signals. To do so would be primarily unfair to Shelby, and totally unjust to those whom she administered. Furthermore, it would disturb the serenity of my own conscience. I prayed for Divine guidance.

Shortly thereafter, I received a phone call from the North Jersey Township Family Service Bureau.

"Mr. Dwyer, would you be interested in having your therapy

dog be an active staff member, visiting shut-ins, schools, as well as assisted living facilities for the elderly?" a deep male voice asked.

"Certainly," I blurted, excited about the proposal. Of course I was interested in having my pup do what she did best—bring joy and comfort to the lonely and suffering. To prohibit Shelby from following her calling would be tantamount to extinguishing the flame of her life's purpose—her *raison d'être*—her reason to be.

"When can we start?"

"Take her in tomorrow—would that work for you?"

"Yes—it's perfect. Shelby and I will come by in the late morning."

Thrilled, I jumped from the chair. Amid such joy, I had to share the moment.

"Shelby, did you hear?" I shouted, though she was seated right beside me. "The Township Family Service Bureau called for you. We're going over tomorrow." From the wide sweep of her tail wag and the gleam in her glance, I knew she shared my excitement.

The following morning, after a leisurely breakfast, quality time with Greta, Rommel and Spartacus and a short walk, Shelby and I left for the Township Family Service Bureau. Upon our arrival, we were met and welcomed by several friendly and gracious individuals, most of whom took an instant liking to my special pup.

However, from the corner of my eye, I noticed that one woman seemed to shy away. Whereas the others crowded around Shelby, petting her head and making small talk, she stood by, a spectator to the scene.

Afterward, she came closer, gently extending her hand to touch Shelby's back.

"You don't have to be afraid," I whispered. "She's very sweet and loves all the attention she can get."

"I don't want to be condescending in any way, but the truth is I was never much of a dog person," she confessed, kneeling over to envelop Shelby in a big hug! "But she is beautiful and has won my affection!"

"I'm not surprised—that's who my pup is," I beamed.

We toured the facility, meeting many diverse people and enjoying the interaction. I provided a brochure complete with Shelby's photo and mine. It detailed her experience, qualifications and information regarding the training completed and therapy dog certification. The brochure offered sufficient data to help them decide if she was suitable to fulfill the 'job' description.

Like an ambassador of good will, Shelby had a smile and a tail wag for everyone who crossed her path. As usual, she was the center of attraction. Much as I was not surprised, I delighted in receiving confirmation.

Towards the end of the visit, I could see she was drained, though she kept pace with the moment, not daring to disappoint or fall short of the expectations placed on her. Refusing to sit, she stood by my side, presenting her congenial face to all.

It seemed as if Shelby was eternally willing to allow the sadness and suffering of others to roam through her own heart, depicting neither a morose mood nor a desire to escape. Hers was a wish to draw off all the negativity in others by letting it flow through her body. This was truly her vocation and she was determined to answer the call with full availability.

That evening, sapped of her energy, Shelby slept like a newborn. Proud and satisfied, I joined her in uninterrupted slumber, but only after having pondered the role of fate and coincidence in daily life. *And what role did redemption play in Shelby's own celebration and triumph from the iniquity endured as an innocent pup?*

At this point it was time for Shelby to gain official status as a therapy dog at the Township Family Service Bureau. By now a shining star, she had the entire community in love with her. Nonetheless, she had to win board approval before she could be instated. It was protocol and had to be followed.

Confident, I awaited the call that would confirm her acceptance.

Several days subsequently, just an hour shy of dinner time, the phone rang.

"Hi, Mr. Dwyer, I'm calling on behalf of the Township Family Service Bureau," a pleasant female voice chimed. "The vote was twenty to two in Shelby's favor—she has been approved as a therapy dog. We are happy to welcome her to the facility."

Though it was the verdict I expected, I was filled with the elation of a surprise victory. Working at the township would truly broaden Shelby's horizons and offer the opportunity to work with children as well as adults of all ages in various institutes and organizations. Justice was finally served—Shelby had earned the right to live her purpose.

But once again, bright, sunny days are sometimes precursors of sinister tempests even when least expected, just as joys every so often unpredictably meander into sadness. In my mind this reversal of fortune is a symptom of the volatility of earthly existence. Not even the beauty of nature is truly gratuitous. Dependent on the sun and rain, it, too, must satisfy a debt.

When the phone rang late on a Friday afternoon, I responded, unaware of the hail storm about to tear through my serenity.

"Mr. Dwyer, I'm from the New Jersey Township Family Service Bureau," a high-pitched female voice announced. "I'm sorry to have to make this phone call, but once the board discovered Shelby is a pit bull, they made a special request for another vote."

I felt my heart drop down to my feet. This could not be good. There was pending doom woven into this message.

"Mr. Dwyer," she continued, nervously clearing her throat, "unfortunately, the favorable decision has been reversed. Pit bulls are categorized as vicious—they have a reputation for violent behavior. I'm sorry, but we cannot take the risk of engaging a ferocious dog—the liability would be overpowering. I'm certain you understand our reasoning for this decision."

Dangerous! Ferocious dog—my sweet, loving Shelby! *Did I hear*

Rommel, Spartacus, Greta and Shelby wish everyone a happy Thanksgiving.

correctly? Was my mild-mannered, gracious pet just labeled 'ferocious'? My empathetic pup who just wants to help those in pain—my mistreated dog who fought an excruciatingly agonizing battle back to health, overcame her own suffering and now wants to give back is allegedly a potential criminal—a threat to frail and debilitated individuals?

Politely I thanked the caller for taking the time to notify me, seizing the moment to express regrets for the mistaken judgment on Shelby's behalf. Believing it best to abstain from any further discussion to maintain my mannerly demeanor, I quickly ended the conversation.

"I'm sorry, Mr. Dwyer," she replied. "You have to understand my hands are tied. It was a board decision."

Unfortunately, I understood the message quite clearly. This was a prime example of the iniquity of racial/ethnic and, in Shelby's case, breed profiling. Based on perhaps prior assumptions or the less-than-pristine reputation of a small minority, generalizations are fabricated and applied to the mainstream.

It is pitifully discriminatory. Sad to say, the existence of prejudicial stereotyping even in the twenty-first century endorses the theory that such biased thinking is seeded with ignorance and irrigated with intolerance.

What hurt most of all was the attributing of a vicious personality to my indulgent and amicable dog without knowledge of who she is. In so doing, thousands of people who would have benefited from her love and compassionate heart would forfeit this bit of solace and companionship due to the errant thinking and grave misconceptions arising from foregone conclusions. Indisputably, this obstinacy to preconceived notions is centered on a shallow mindset that either favors unawareness or deeds done through wickedness.

Unpretentious and effortlessly accommodating, Shelby just wanted to share the generosity of her spirit with others in need of a tender, patient companion.

I opted not to tell Shelby about the discriminatory verdict for fear of hurting her sensitive feelings. Since she possessed neither intolerance in her heart nor bias toward any living creature, she would not understand the rankling existence of prejudice. Furthermore, with her "love thy neighbor as thy self" motto, she would never be able to comprehend the inability of human beings to judge canine character.

I questioned, *Wasn't mankind created intellectually superior to animals?Does this theory need to be revisited and put in proper context?* The last inquiry I left unanswered.

Nevertheless, it is harrowing to note just how deep the slings and arrows of discrimination can pierce and how much pain can result. On the negative side, ignorance is a deleterious malady. But, thankfully, on the positive side, there is a cure.

That evening I observed Shelby as she played with Rommel, Greta and Spartacus. Though more than double their size, her graceful gentleness dominated their antics. She was an apparition of everything kind and placid. It was apparent she was far from vicious. My heart was broken over the great injustice in her regard, especially since it was so undeserving.

To compensate, I lavished her with extra love and praise, hoping she would not pick up on my demoralized spirit. Passive and serene, she stood before me, her big, glowing eyes brimming over with unconditional love. Like a consenting martyr accepting the Lord's will, she did not contest her fate.

My mind drifted as I continued to follow her while, lithe and swift-footed, she scurried around the room.

"Joe," Geralynn's voice interrupted my thoughts, "I still can't believe the Township Family Services Bureau turned Shelby away."

"It's absurd—totally unreal. Do you remember the day in Rochelle Park when that young woman sprang from behind, squeezed Shelby's face and bit her nose?"

"Yes, I recall."

"Well, although she turned to me with a puzzled look, the love in her heart never faded from her gaze. Geralynn, am I nuts? Shelby did not even defend herself against an unknown aggressor! Is this the profile of a vicious dog?"

"Joe, you are not nuts—quite the contrary. This proves the threatening power of ignorance. It mangles and deforms the truth in the minds of those who wallow in it."

"Yes, and, more importantly, it confirms Shelby's greatness. Despite the rejection and unjust condemnation, she has neither anger nor revenge in her heart. Look at the sweetness in her face.

Completely irresistible.

She has forgiven them just as she has forgiven the transgression of mankind in her regard—no excuses requested."

Although Shelby had returned from the day's missionary visit exhausted, drained and with an upset stomach, which was more usual than unusual, she slept like an infant. Selflessly giving of herself to comfort and assist those in pain does cost her. However, willingness to sacrifice her own well-being for that of others defines who Shelby is.

What matters to my sweet pup is not what was done unto her yesterday but what she can do today to make the lives of others a bit more bearable and serene, even if not joyful. Though she has drawn many smiles from faces knotted in pain, Shelby never questions—she only responds.

Clear of conscience and pure of intent, my pup enjoyed a well-merited rest. Plagued with disappointment and an unshakeable, melancholic frustration, I instead danced the restless steps of the insomnia tango.

Scooter's Great-Nephew— *The Jeff Rizzuto Story Part I*

"Dogs are our link to paradise. They don't know evil or jealousy or discontent. To sit with a dog on a hillside on a glorious afternoon is to be back in Eden, where doing nothing was not boring, it was peace."

—Milan Kundera

Though a firm disbeliever in Friedrich Nietzsche's atheistic theories, I have to admit that his summation of the after-effects of human pain and conflict stated simply as *"what doesn't kill us makes us stronger"* has been repeatedly validated in my life. Interestingly, a prime example of empowerment through hardship is clearly evidenced in the vicissitudes of Shelby's experience.

Judging from the severity of her injuries, her early months had to be a hell on earth with consequences that seeded and developed in her an extraordinary, almost inexplicable compassion and empathy for those in distress. Moreover, as if her physical torments were insufficient hardships, now discrimination had been added to the list. However, unlike her injured legs, this type of mistreatment labeled 'prejudice' is in a sense a faceless malady. Yet despite its invisible nature and drug-resistant prognosis, the wounds inflicted throb and sting with the same intensity of a physical hurt. Healing, however, is not the result of medication but an unleashing of the power within—a power more potent than tablets, capsules, injections and infusions, a power with neither noxious side effects nor potential for failure.

Precisely, this is how Shelby gained the strength needed to rise above the adversity and oppression she was saddled with during her first year of life. And this is how she overcame the virtually caustic effects of an iniquitous, knowledge-starved bias.

Eventually, absorbing my unexpressed sadness and disappointment, she learned of the prejudice in her regard demonstrated by the North Jersey Township Bureau. Much as I struggled for the words to explain to Shelby why certain individuals remain trapped in preconceived notions, basing judgments and decisions on distorted and tendentious anecdotal evidence, she seemed to already understand, flashing me a '*don't worry, Dad, I'll get through this also and be a better dog afterward*' response!

In that moment I became aware of Shelby's stateliness and maturity. All that my pup had endured truly strengthened her character, giving her deeper, more insightful perspectives on life. Undoubtedly, she was wise beyond her years and species—though there is room for debate on the latter concept.

These unfavorable circumstances fortified her disposition and garnered her resistance both in the light of daily disappointments and worse. Undeniably, the rigors of her experience had sharpened my pup's coping skills. Not only an A-student in the school of 'hard knocks,' she quickly stepped into the role of lecturer.

Shelby taught me it was time to quit wasting precious energy on the negative and focus instead on the positive, which was certainly a great deal more productive—something over which we had control. Humbly, I let my pet teach me an important life lesson—clear of mind, loving of heart, walk forward—never backward. There were moments in which I could swear she gazed at me with the wisdom and astuteness I had not yet seen in an illustrious professor emeritus.

Most days, the sun rises at dawn and sets in the evenings. Occasionally, catastrophe tests man's endurance and faith. Now and then it storms. Nature's cathartic screams burst into tears. According to the Lord's will, the sky clears, the sun blazes and nature enjoys the serenity of post-release.

For mankind, similar cycles influence our lives, creating havoc and gifting joy. Sometimes we feel the paralyzing gloom of defeat. Other times, weary from it all, we are jolted by the rejuvenating surge of a difficult triumph. Always we continue the journey.

Thankful for the blessings I had received since I had adopted Shelby from the shelter, I prayed she would be able to answer the Lord's call. *Please let someone in need benefit from my pup's beautiful, nurturing presence,* I'd pray daily. *Please let me witness the birth of a genuine smile on the face of an oppressed and lonely person when Shelby's paw rests on a hurting knee.* Then I surrendered her mission to God—*Thy will be done!*

Several days thereafter, while leisurely browsing through the newspaper, I received a phone call from Brenna, the wife of a dear friend, Jeff Rizzuto. Quickly flipping through my mind, I paused at the memory of the day I had officiated at their wedding, joyfully pronouncing the beautiful, so-much-in-love young couple "man and wife," after their vows had been tearfully spoken.

My eyes still mist at the vision of Jeff and Brenna exchanging their first, lingering, almost embarrassing 'altar' kiss as Mr. and Mrs. Beyond endearing, the rosy flush of their cheeks was delicately sweet.

Several years later I brought their two sons into the Catholic faith, christening each newborn in due time as Brenna and Jeff stood at the baptismal font, alongside the handpicked godparents, joyful witnesses to the purification of their children's souls.

A tall, athletic gentleman, handsome of countenance, still athletic of build, Jeff was a committed family man. His ancestry boasted New York Yankees short-stop Phil Rizutto of the Baseball Hall of Fame. One of the best bunters in history, the 'Scooter,' as

Mr. Rizutto was good-humoredly nicknamed, was known to Jeff
as 'Uncle Phil.'

Needless to say, be it finely wired in his DNA or just a coinci-
dental factor, Jeff not only had a compelling passion for baseball,
but was a die-hard Yankee fan. Nothing, not even the devastating
cancer diagnosis he received in 2005, could dampen his enthusiasm when the team was on the baseball diamond, mitts, bats and
ball in hand. I doubt he ever missed a game in all his thirty-eight
years. The New York Yankees were in his blood, an uncompromis-
ing circumstance of life second only to God and his family.

Jeff underwent several rounds of rigorous, energy-sapping
chemotherapy treatments for the cancer in his spine until his
oncologist confirmed the good news of a much prayed for remis-
sion. With two children of tender age and a young wife, Jeff found
a calamitous threat like cancer devastatingly overwhelming to
accept, let alone digest.

*Would Jeff's sons understand why their dad was sometimes too
exhausted to play with them? Would they think he was not interested—would they feel abandoned? Could they possibly comprehend
in their still underdeveloped minds why he would sometimes sit,
drained of all force, barely able to speak? Were they too young to
grasp how frayed and worn the thread holding their dad's life truly
was? Did they know the meaning of death?*

Much as I wanted to assist Jeff—to help alleviate some of the
pain and anguish of his situation—I felt powerless whenever we
parted company. All I could do was bow my head in prayer.

It was January 5, and I will never forget the desperate wea-
riness in Brenna's voice. Something in her raspy 'hello' sent my
pulse racing.

"Joe," she said, pausing. "I'm afraid I have some bad news."

"Are the boys okay?" I blurted, always fearful of the misfor-
tunes befalling the innocent.

"The children are fine. But I'm afraid Jeff's cancer is back. This
time it has metastasized."

"That doesn't sound good. Will he have to face another round of chemo?"

"No, the doctors said he's terminal. It has spread from his spine throughout the body. All they can do for him is continue dialysis to keep his blood purified and administer pain medication. Joe, it's just a matter of time. The doctors have done all they could for Jeff. Medical science can no longer offer any hope for healing. It's now in the Lord's hands. Only a miracle could save Jeff."

"I'm so sorry, Brenna," I said, realizing she was quietly weeping. "I'll come by to see him in the afternoon if it's okay. Please ask Jeff if he's up for a visit."

"Sure, Joe, Jeff would love to see you! I don't even have to ask. And I would appreciate it also."

In despair, people become exceedingly more faith-dependent—sometimes it's comparable to a knee-jerk reaction. I hung up the phone, struggled to catch my breath, rested my chin on tightly clasped hands that trembled ever so slightly and put Jeff's fate in the Lord's heart.

While I had the Divine Ear, I begged to be of service to Jeff, perhaps rendering his transition more serene while guiding his thoughts and feelings as he sought closure with family and preparation to meet his Creator. Mine was not an easy mission. Nonetheless, still unaware of the power within my inspirational assistant, who had come through for me in the past, I was unknowing of just how far-reaching and intense Shelby's ability to comfort not only Jeff but his whole family would be!

After lunch, as promised, I cleared my schedule and headed over to the Rizzutos'. Gracious and welcoming, Brenna accompanied me to the living room, where Jeff was seated, zapping the remote.

"What are you looking for...a Yankees game?" I teased. "This is still football season—we're at the playoffs for the Super Bowl."

Although it warmed my heart to see Jeff's lips part in a huge smile, I questioned if I would have the strength and ability to be

Sweet girl o' mine.

a source of comfort and inspiration during the difficult months ahead. Powerless to heal the ills of my friend's weakening body, I knew I had to help him defend his faith from the slings and arrows of despair and a pitiful 'why me' mindset so enticing in desperate moments. *Were my goals attainable?* Jeff was a man of faith, but would he be triumphant in his last earthly battle?

"Joe, so what's been keeping you busy?" Jeff asked, shutting off the TV.

"The usual—family, work, the dogs," I responded. Taking a deep breath, I continued, introducing my fabulous therapy dog, Shelby.

"Then there's Shelby," I said, with pomp and grandeur, as if I were announcing the birth of a new infant daughter.

Once I had fully captured Jeff and Brenna's attention, interest and curiosity, I related Shelby's story, beginning with the genesis of her abuse, abandonment at the gas station, shelter internment, adoption and painful surgery to rectify her serious crippling leg issues.

As I spoke, their eyes widened, almost in disbelief. Theirs was an unconscious skepticism too strong to conceal even for the sake of friendship and good breeding. Seizing the moment, I paused before delivering the update on my pup's life.

"Is Shelby okay now?" Jeff asked, my misty eyes obviously betraying the special relationship I shared with my beloved pit bull.

"'Okay' is a great understatement," I blurted. "I didn't finish the story. Shortly thereafter, Shelby was trained and certified as a therapy dog! She's absolutely awe-inspiring with people, in spite of the initial maltreatment and rejection. Everyone just loves her. They say she brings joy to all, in particular those who suffer. Shelby seems to have the insights of a human being and the empathy of a saint. It is mind-boggling to witness her in action, tending to individuals with physical and emotional disabilities, issues and handicaps."

From the way in which Brenna put down her coffee cup and pushed it away, as if the steamy, aromatic brew no longer delighted her taste buds, I knew my Shelby, though still unknown to husband and wife, had intrigued my hosts—and why not? She was truly extraordinary. Serving others was a meaningful vocation for Shelby—a mission she took seriously, pouring her heart and soul into giving her all physically and emotionally.

"That's quite a story," Jeff interjected as I rose to my feet, unwilling to needlessly tire my ailing friend. "Shelby is lucky to have you."

Smiling, I nodded, protecting behind tightly locked lips the secret held within. The truth is I was the fortunate one. Freed from the shackles of my own depression, I, too, was rescued from what could have been a bitter, tragic fate—rescued by Shelby. It was proof that what goes around comes around.

Returning home, I thought of Jeff and his family. They had a physically and emotionally strenuous journey to complete. *God, I* prayed, *please use me to soften the thorny paths ahead. Please allow me to lead Brenna and the boys to serene acceptance, and guide Jeff to his final destination—heaven.*

An hour after dinner, as I was settling myself to unwind and watch some TV before retiring, the phone rang.

"Joe," Brenna said delicately, "Jeff enjoyed your visit today. Thanks for stopping by. It meant a lot to us. He felt uplifted, loved the story about Shelby, ate a nice dinner and is resting comfortably."

"It was my pleasure, Brenna. I wish I could do more."

"Actually, you can," she said. "Jeff and I would love it if you took Shelby with you on your next visit! After hearing her inspiring story, we're eager to meet her."

I was ecstatic—it seemed as if a handsome Prince Charming had just galloped up my driveway on a white horse to request my daughter's hand in marriage!

Shelby's Grand Slam—
The Jeff Rizzuto Story Part II

"Shelby has been and is a true gift from God. She has brought such peace and comfort not only to Jeff during his terrible illness and passing but to me and my children every time we see her. She's extraordinary!"

—Brenna Rizzuto

Before resting the sports section of the paper on the coffee table for my son to pick up, I thumbed through one more time, hoping my eyes would fall on a scheduled Yankees game. Shelby sat quietly across the room; on her countenance was stamped anticipation and the unknown expectation of a new day still to be defined.

Spotting the announcement of a game, I read it aloud, excited. My pup rose to her feet, her expression changing abruptly as she came to my side. *Did she understand the reason for my sudden burst of enthusiasm? Did she know that Jeff was truly gravely ill and that watching the New York Yankees would distract his mind from the tragic inevitable while lifting his spirits?*

I left my queries unanswered until Shelby fixed her gaze on mine. At that point it was obvious—any response would have been merely just a waste of time. I knew she understood. But, more importantly, I knew she was questioning, *"When are we going to see Jeff?*" Apparently, a bond had been formed. Furthermore, passionate about the welfare of those in distress and committed to her mission, she felt an overwhelming inclination to be of service. This is who she is and she had little choice but to honor her essence.

"Joe, I noticed the Yankees are playing this evening," Geralynn shouted from the kitchen. That should cheer up Jeff a bit."

"Yes, I saw that in the paper. Shelby and I are planning an early afternoon visit. I already phoned Brenna. This will give Jeff some time to rest and have dinner before Vázquez throws the first pitch."

"I'm so happy it's baseball season—perfect timing." Geralynn sounded so genuinely relieved. We were both exceedingly worried about Jeff and his young family. To witness, powerless but resigned, a loved one pass away at thity-nine years of age is excruciatingly painful, especially for children, who still lack a full understanding of death.

"Me, too," I blurted. "It's a great distraction. I asked Brenna if two-ish would work and she immediately said yes."

"I can see Shelby is ready to go right now," Geralynn said, walking into the room. Smiling quietly, I realized she noticed the urgency and readiness in Shelby's demeanor.

I nodded, confirming the accuracy of her consideration. After all, it was blatantly obvious. Unlike mankind, sometimes given to emotional subterfuge and subtle game-playing, Shelby was virtuously honest and open about her feelings—no intrigues, no secrets, no hidden agendas. She wore her heart across her forehead for anyone and everyone to see.

Both Shelby and I were silent and reflective during the ride over to Jeff's. Between us there existed a special complicity never in need of verbal communication. It was a look, a sudden physical proximity and a quietness that spoke volumes.

Spotting the Rizzuto mailbox, I gradually tapped the brake. My pup bolted upright.

"We're here, Shelby," I said, gazing at her in my rearview mirror.

As soon as I opened the door, she was out, her tail wagging, brimming over with healing energy. Brenna was at the door, waiting to greet us.

"Hi, Joe—hi, Shelby," she sang, visibly excited to see us. "Jeff's waiting to meet you, Shelby!"

The Rizzutos' extended family included four cats. At first apprehensive, I hoped all the negative hype about cats and dogs was just hearsay. Regardless, I held my breath until after the initial impact and investigative sniffing on Shelby's part. Calm prevailed. Thankfully, all five behaved as ambassadors of peace and goodwill. It is assumed either their feline intuition was tuned in or their IQs are higher than man approximated.

Brenna was instantly mesmerized by Shelby's warm, charismatic personality. Sliding into a genuflection, she cradled Shelby's face in her hands.

"You're beautiful," she cooed, kissing the top of her head. "You have no idea how happy I am to see you."

Proud papa stood by beaming!

"Come on, Shelby, I want you to meet Jeff," Brenna said, leading the way to the living room. I could see she was already more relaxed. My pup had worked some of her magic!

I trailed behind Brenna and Shelby until we reached the living room. As always, the house was spotless. Welcoming and cozy, it was not merely a sheltering refuge from the elements. Instead, it said much about the people who lived within its core. It spoke of a family united. It spoke of love.

"Jeff, this is Shelby," she said, casting an adoring glance at her spouse. "Shelby, this is my husband, Jeff."

I felt my eyes fill up. Meanwhile, Shelby turned, looked at me briefly then focused her gaze on Jeff. Observing the scenario as a bystander, I noticed her face change as if the sudden obsession to comfort him was an urgent destiny—her destiny, a lot over which she had no control.

Jeff seemed equally enthralled, his eyes glued to Shelby.

"Joe, she's absolutely gorgeous," he blurted. "She's everything I heard and more! Thanks so much for bringing her here." His words were more emotional than complimentary. It was a done deal—I knew Shelby had won the heart of another gentleman.

With slow, graceful movements unhampered by the shyness of unfamiliarity and the newness of their just-begun relationship, Shelby climbed up on the sofa to be near Jeff. My heart pounded—I questioned if perhaps she was overstepping her boundary. *Was she being too presumptuous? Did they feel at ease with her invading their space? Should I intervene?*

And while I stewed, wasting precious energy, Shelby inched herself up closer to Jeff.

"I'm sorry," I murmured apologetically, walking over to the sofa. "I had no idea she would…"

"Oh, no, no, no—she's sweet and loving," Jeff interrupted, his face brightening. "Don't you dare take her away." Encircling his arms around Shelby, he gave her a hug. "She's a darling—I absolutely love her!"

Although Shelby had never put a paw down in the Rizzuto house, she seemed amazingly at home. This was a new experience for me because even though she knew my parents quite well and had been to their home on numerous occasions, she continued to move about hesitatingly, as if she were sailing in uncharted seas. Behaving more like a guest than a family member, she repeatedly looked to me for permission before changing her position. Sometimes I got the impression she felt like an uncertain ten-year-old, afraid to disobey a parental order.

Shelby stayed near Jeff, attached to his body for quite some time. He doted on her, caressing her soft, silky fur, smiling and reciprocating her charming coyness. Time sped along, yet no one seemed to mind or care.

When I gazed down at my watch, I suddenly realized how long our visit had become. I feared overtiring Jeff and perhaps interrupting family plans for the afternoon.

"Shelby, I think it's time to go," I said, actually feeling bad about ending a beautiful interlude. "Say goodbye to Jeff and Brenna."

Lifting her head, Shelby gave Jeff a quick, neat lick on the chin. He was radiant!

"Will you come back to see me again?" he asked, locking his arms around her neck.

"Sure, Jeff," I said, "whenever you wish. Just have Brenna give me a call."

Once again, with the grace of a prima ballerina and the compassion of Mother Theresa, Shelby climbed off the sofa. Understanding Jeff was gravely ill, and having experienced firsthand the atrocity of pain, she tried her best to be neither abrupt nor jarring for fear of adding to his discomfort.

As Shelby distanced herself from her new friend, she turned several times to cast him a nurturing glance. It seemed as if she were departing company from her child on the first day of kindergarten. With a flirtatious wag of the tail in Jeff's full view, she walked into the entry foyer, swinging her taught *derrière*.

"I don't know how to thank you," Brenna said, breathless, leaning over to give my pup a goodbye kiss. "That was absolutely awesome. Honestly, I don't know if I would have given this much credibility to Shelby had I not been present in the room. For sure, the allure of her charisma is irresistible."

During the short ride home, Shelby's motionless body filled the back seat, totally sapped of energy—an energy she had generously imparted to Jeff. I knew that in spite of the extreme exhaustion, my pup was feeling the exhilaration of having brought comfort and a bit of joy to a dying man.

That evening, shortly before bedtime, Brenna phoned.

"Joe, I hope I'm not disturbing you by calling at this hour. I wanted to wait for Jeff to settle down and fall asleep."

"Not at all, Brenna," I responded. "You can call me anytime. Is everything okay?"

"'Okay' is an understatement, Joe. That's why I'm phoning. Shelby was beyond belief. Jeff was feeling discouraged today. He just picked at his lunch and seemed listless, as if he was just giving up. Though he didn't complain of pain, he was depressed. I knew he was focusing on his compromised fate. It saddened me because I felt so powerless."

"I know how you're feeling; it's awful to see someone you love suffering and not be able to do anything about it."

"Well, after Shelby left, Jeff jumped off the sofa and inquired what was for dinner. Best of all, he ate with delight—everything, leaving behind not even a crumb. It was like he had a sudden jolt of energy!"

"That's wonderful."

"Yes. Joe, this was Shelby's doing—she's an angel. I can't believe the effect she had on Jeff."

"Brenna, your words fill me with joy, even though I'm not surprised. I think Shelby has a very special feeling for Jeff—she senses he is afflicted with suffering. She knows he's needy and she wants to fill that need. This is who she is."

"Incredible—this is incredible, Joe."

"I know—so please don't hesitate to call whenever Jeff's up for a visit."

"How about Thursday?" Brenna blurted, chuckling.

"We'll make it work," I responded, happy to hear her animated laugh.

At last Shelby had come into her own persona. Able to embrace the power within, she experienced a different happiness—the melancholic happiness of giving a dying man a moment of joy.

Jeff was undergoing long and tedious dialysis at the hospital several times a week. Often Brenna was anxious and concerned and asked if Shelby could stop by for a quick, reassuring visit. She found comfort with my pup while Jeff was away from home. The

Ready for action.

unpredictable nature of his precarious fate troubled her. But in Shelby she found an empathetic friend, a confidante able and willing to soothe her nerves.

By now Shelby was part of the Rizzuto family. Whenever Shelby entered the residence, she would head directly for the sofa where Jeff usually sat. We all knew where her loyalty rested. Finding his seat vacant, she would turn, approach Brenna and settle down snugly at her feet, gazing up with nurturing eyes to be certain her pal was calm.

A being of extraordinary sensibility complete with an inner network of elaborate emotions touching human level, Shelby had an aura that lit up the house. Her charisma kindled even the most consumed wicks. Her presence settled the most restless souls. Like a best friend whose silent words speak louder than the piercing echoes of a screaming crowd, she quietly communicated her love and solidarity.

Shelby was addictive! During one visit with Jeff, Brenna asked if she could stay a bit longer.

"Joe, the boys have heard so much about Shelby—she's all Jeff and I talk about. I'd like them to meet her. Do you think she would like that?"

"Sure, Shelby loves children."

"They should be here in about a half hour."

Hearing about our prolonged visit, Shelby agreed to remain attached to Jeff's hip for a longer period. In reciprocity, Jeff flashed a full-toothed smile. My heart warmed and the words of Stephen Grellet, the French Quaker missionary, came to mind: *"I expect to pass through this world but once. Any good, therefore, that I can do or any kindness I can show to any fellow creature, let me do it now..."* This seemed to be Shelby's philosophy of life, a belief system she honored unfailingly.

The sound of childish giggles jolted me upright from my slouched position. Jeff and Brenna's sons, Jake, eight, and Alex, five, were returning from school. My mind faltered, though by now

I should have known better. *Would the boys like Shelby? Would she have the same dazzling effect on them as she did on their mom and dad? Would Shelby love them as she did their parents?*

I didn't have much time to dwell either on doubts or questions. In a heartbeat, both boys were in the living room, chattering in unison, one out-shouting the other for attention while depositing kisses on their parents' cheeks.

Shelby waited patiently, until the curtain had fallen on the opening scene, before making a move.

"Jake, Alex, this is the famous Shelby that your mom and I talk about," Jeff beamed, stroking her back. "Isn't she beautiful?"

Like a leading lady, head high, Shelby stepped off the sofa and flirtatiously sauntered over to Jake. Though unafraid, he had both the rigid posture of a child about to meet a new companion and the uncertain gaze that asked 'will she like me'?

Alex, only five, was a bit more nonchalant, though he, too, somewhat embroiled in the hesitancy of unfamiliarity, kept a motionless stance. Unfamiliarity more often than not breeds insecurity. However, it didn't take much—a look into Jake's eyes and two sniffs. Shyly, Shelby licked the back of his hand as he lifted his arm to caress her back.

Secure she had made a friend, Shelby moved over to his little brother. Another glance—this time in Alex's eyes—followed by two short sniffs, and it was a done deal. Confirmation of friendship—one quick lick under the chin as he bent over to pat her head.

Taking a few steps back, Shelby stood, observing the Rizzuto brothers. Certain of her own feelings for the boys, she wondered if her comradeship was reciprocated.

"She's awesome," Jake giggled. Both boys reached out to her, throwing their arms around her. From the wild wag of her tail, I knew she was thrilled.

"Yea," Alex chimed in. "I like her because she didn't lick all over my face."

For a five-year-old, Alex was perceptive and had made an excellent observation. It was true—much as Shelby was extroverted and loving, she neither demonstrated her ardor with a barrage of wet, sticky licks and kisses nor stood up, placing her front paws on someone. Yet despite her thoughtful behavior, she made it more than obvious her feelings were deep and intense. Gracious and congenial, she never relaxes her courteous conduct. She is a true lady, refined though passionate, polished though emotionally involved, and always accommodating.

Although Shelby fell in love with Jake and Alex that day, and although it was a triumphant grand slam at the Rizzuto house, the apple of her eye remained Jeff. Jeff needed her; therefore, Shelby never strayed more than a minute or two from his side.

Shelby's Broken Heart— Goodbye, Jeff

"Shelby is very special. I think God chose her to accept the pain she went through because He knew she could handle it and now look at what great things she is doing. I think He also chose me since He believes I can handle the pain I have. I want to do some positive things as well."
—Jeff Rizzuto, 1970-2010

Shelby continued to visit Jeff on a regular basis, never failing to draw smiles on his wasted face and brighten his ever-increasingly pale complexion. By now the suffering in his eyes was difficult to witness by family and those who loved him. His energy quickly seeping away was a nemesis to his daily activities and his hope for a second redemption.

Shelby monitored Jeff's slips and slides, giving more love and comfort as his strong, young body weakened. Once she fell in love, there was no turning back. She was nurturing and empathetic, and he was her charge; she took seriously her therapy dog mothering. A veteran of pain and suffering, Shelby knew the right approach and the appropriate words, lovingly communicated through her sweet gaze and the most efficient nuzzling strategies to soothe any discomfort. In just a few short months, she had become a master.

I, of course, was thrilled my pup was performing salubrious corporal works of mercy. Nevertheless, though subtle in her ministry, Shelby was gaining fame in the neighborhood. Parishioners started to speak about her—and soon after I would meet others in diverse locales.

"Joe, we saw Shelby's picture—she's beautiful," they'd say teasingly. "We also heard she's phenomenal with people in difficulty! We'll keep that in mind." Eventually, when introduced to people I did not know personally, I'd be surprised to hear: "We know you and we know who Shelby is! We've heard so much about her! She's a celebrity around here."

Though puzzled at first, I soon learned that Brenna had snapped photos of Shelby, which she uploaded on her cell phone. Whenever anyone inquired about Jeff's well-being, she would pull out her phone, tell of Shelby's special powers and show the photos. Eventually Shelby was asked to be her friend on Facebook. Thus, the mystery was resolved! For me it was inspiring to learn what an impact my pup had made on so many people, and her therapy dog career was only in the initial stages. *How far would my trailblazing pit bull travel?Just how much pain and anguish would she carry on her back to comfort others?*

The shrill ring of the phone trumped my thoughts.

"Joe, I'm phoning from the hospital," Brenna said, sighing. "Jeff was admitted about twenty minutes ago." Her voice was laced with concern, an accentuated unease too penetrating not to take seriously.

"Joe, do you think you can come over with Shelby? I know Jeff would love it—and she does him so much good. He's a different man after her visit—like before he got sick."

In spite of my apprehension over Jeff's worsening condition, Brenna's words brought a mass invasion of goose bumps along the perimeters of my lower arms. The look of pride on my face was probably too indisputable not to merit credibility.

Standing in the doorway, Geralynn gave testimony to my own consideration. Realizing I was speaking with Brenna, she retained her breath and her words until after I placed the receiver in the cradle.

"Geralynn, Jeff has been readmitted. He must have suffered a crisis."

"Why don't you go over with Shelby? I'm sure both Jeff and Brenna would feel comforted by a visit."

"Exactly my plan—but I'll have to speak with administration first to see if Shelby will get permission. She has never served in a hospital before, so I don't know what the protocol is."

I summoned my angel of mercy, and we drove over to the renowned Hackensack University Medical Center, a 202-year-old teaching hospital with a well-known reputation for excellence in healthcare, not only in Bergen County, but in the nation. Hackensack had made the top hospitals list and was cited in the November 20, 2006, *New York Magazine* among the ten best facilities for cancer, cardio, gastroenterology, orthopedics, obstetrics/gynecology, pediatrics and emergency services. Jeff was in good hands.

Adrenalin was rushing through my veins like a gushing oil well. I felt as if I had just consumed a double espresso after running the New York marathon! If only Shelby would be granted permission to enter—it would be a groundbreaking moment for her career, not to mention the good she would do.

Pulling up to the entry, I searched for guest parking. Instantly, Shelby sat up. I prayed I would not have to disappoint her. In my excitement, I had failed to remember that Jeff was in dialysis; therefore, Brenna had not yet arrived. Gazing at my watch, I realized we had about an hour's wait.

Since it was a lovely early April day, I took advantage of the pleasurable climate to stand outside and bask in the warming rays of the sun. A soft breeze just barely rustled the trees as several swarms of birds flew overhead in shadowy, gliding waves. Though idyllic, the sweetness of the spring air was marred by the fumes of gasoline as cars pulled up in droves, either to discharge or collect passengers and guests.

Seated beside me, enjoying the tickling breeze on her face, Shelby had eyes that glowed with the anticipation of spending time with Jeff. Every so often she would shift from side to side, her eagerness interrupting the calm. I caught myself mimicking her nervous movements.

But never would I have anticipated the attention she received within a forty-five-minute time span. Every person entering or leaving the hospital stopped to pet or have a word with her—even visibly exhausted physicians and nurses, coming off twelve-hour shifts.

Oozing charisma, Shelby seemed to attract them all—young and elderly, male and female, children and teens. Bent at the waist, kneeling, squatting—every position was legitimate to make eye contact. Composed and professional, though open and loving, Shelby was available and gracious. Just being herself, without serving, brought the multitude to her—she had to be cast from a very special mold.

Later that evening, folding my napkin after dinner, I would thank Geralynn for her excellent menu and tell her about the people I had met while standing outside the hospital. "Where was Shelby when I was single?" I'd say, laughing. "Women sure did flock to her."

Geralynn would take it good-naturedly, smiling.

"Well, Joe," she'd blurt, "didn't Fritz give his approval? Didn't you ask his opinion about me?"

Geralynn would raise a valid point. Yet despite the teasing, I'd realize God did not send me Shelby during my bachelor days simply because I was more than capable of meeting and marrying a truly wonderful girl. Therefore, He knew I did not require any assistance. Furthermore, Shelby's purpose in life was to be far more meaningful than playing cupid.

I gave my watch another hurried glance. "Just about fifteen minutes more," I said to Shelby. "I think we'll give Jeff some time to settle in and let Brenna get here." A wag of her tail told me she was in agreement.

Time is sometimes an illusion. We can't grasp it, yet it exists in our minds, influencing our lives. Before I could recollect my thoughts, a dark car drove into the entry area. The sun's reflection on the windows obscured my view. Squinting to shadow some of the glare, I focused on the driver. However, when the door opened, I noticed the passenger was a rather elderly lady, well dressed though slight of stature and rather frail.

Immediately, Shelby's gaze dove in her direction. Then in the snap of a finger, it settled on mine with a questioning look. I, too, wondered if perhaps she was in need of assistance.

"Mom, wait a minute, I'm coming around to help you," a female voice echoed from the driver's seat. I breathed a sigh of relief, though I would not have hesitated to escort her wherever she wished to go.

Struggling a bit, the woman stood outside the car just as the wind kicked up, ruffling her tightly curled white hair. I seized the opportunity to fill my lungs with a few whips of cool air, all without interrupting my focus.

Once on her feet, the elderly lady staggered over to Shelby.

A full-figured, middle-aged woman of average height jumped from the car and ran over to her side.

"You should have waited for me, Mom," she admonished sweetly. "You could have fallen—you're shaking. Let's go inside."

"No, I want to see this dog," she responded firmly. All the strength absent in her body was present in her voice and in her resolve.

Shelby's animated tail-wagging was an obvious non-verbal exclamation of joy. I knew my pup's magnetism had enchanted again—there was certainly a connection.

While the elderly woman stood smiling at Shelby, I broke the silence. "Madam, would you like to meet her?" I asked, motioning to my pup with my right hand.

The sudden gleam in her eyes led me to follow suit. "This is Shelby," I said proudly. "She's a therapy dog."

"Shelby's beautiful...absolutely beautiful. I'm so happy I met her. I feel so much better! Everything is going to be just fine."

A pale, gnarled, tremulous hand reached out to touch Shelby's face. Immediately, three sets of eyes glowed then welled—hers, mine and Shelby's. It was a special moment of service. I'm certain my pup's heart was beating as rapidly as mine.

All together, in less than an hour, we had encountered over thirty people—all drawn to Shelby's magnetism and charming presence. She seemed to literally pull people to her.

"Okay, Shelby, you made another fan," I said, chuckling. "Now let's go see Jeff."

Once inside the hospital, I walked over to the reception desk, automatically confiscating the doubts that until now had been playing tag in my stomach.

"God, this has to work," I whispered under my breath—*"for Shelby and for Jeff. I know this is part of Your plan."*

"Hello, how may I help you?" a young woman said from behind the counter.

"I'm Joe Dwyer, and this is Shelby," I replied. "She's a certified therapy dog—we're here to see Jeff Rizzuto." Gently I slid Shelby's certification papers across the counter. It never hurts to present 'evidence.'

She gave a quick read, gazed at Shelby and smiled. "Do you know Mr. Rizzuto's room number?"

"Yes, thank you—I've been to see him before."

"Have a nice day."

My pulse raced. This was Shelby's maiden hospital visit as a therapy dog. A new chapter was about to be written!

We trotted off to the elevator en route to Jeff's room. When the door opened, I motioned for Shelby to follow me into the corridor. Echoes of surgeons saving lives, doctors healing the sick and nurses tending to the needy sent Shelby's ears into an erect position. Playfully, I scratched the top of her head; she reciprocated with a loving glance. There were never lapses in our connection.

"I think Jeff is at the end of the hall," I whispered. We continued our stroll until we reached his room.

"Mr. Rizzuto is still in dialysis," a tall, handsome, surfer-type assistant said, showing a full set of pearly white teeth. Shelby's attention suddenly focused in his direction. *Was I jealous of her coy, flirtatious antics?*

"We will wait here until he returns," I muttered, distracting her gaze.

As we stood outside Jeff's door, I heard a female voice from directly across the hall.

"I don't care what you say, Mom. I'm going out there to see that dog."

Suddenly the door swung wide open. A middle-aged woman dressed in a hospital gown approached.

"Can I spend some time with that dog?" she asked, her eyes glued on my pup.

"Absolutely—her name is Shelby."

"Hi, Shelby," she said, cuddling my pet's face between her hands. "It's so nice to have you here." I, of course, was ecstatic. If I ever needed confirmation of Shelby's charm and charisma, I was getting it today.

"Thank you so much."

I assumed the woman's mother was concerned when her daughter bolted over to Shelby, but when she saw the look of solace on her daughter's face, she had to realize how beneficial my pup's presence was for her daughter in that particular moment.

Within minutes, Jeff's family arrived: Brenna, his parents and an uncle.

"This is the famous Shelby we always talk about," Brenna said, leaning over to kiss her. "She is our little angel."

We exchanged a few words. When I felt a pull on Shelby's leash, I turned just in time to see Jeff wheeled down the corridor on a stretcher. Her signal stiffened me, much as I tried to conceal my concern.

"Hi," Jeff said hoarsely, his ashen face a portrait of suffering. As the stretcher disappeared into the room, I felt another tug on the leash.

"Just a minute, Shelby. Let's wait until Jeff is comfortable in bed." She obeyed, though I'd bet reluctantly.

As soon as we entered, Shelby, like a graceful dolphin riding the waves, tried to float up onto the bed. Unfortunately, much as Jeff protested, her attempt had to be aborted due to the tubes and machines to which he was attached. However, determined, she put into action plan B. Standing on her two hind legs, she rested her front paws on the bed near his shoulders, settling her face on the side of Jeff's chin. He tilted his head to make eye contact. Suddenly all 250 myths in Ovid's *Metamorphoses* paled.

His countenance, drained of color, his brow, thickly knitted in pain, his smile, faint and forced, his demeanor, listless—kissed away with two licks. Even more striking was the delicate pink flush on his hallowed cheeks, the relaxed network of lines boldly scratched across his forehead and the glow of a genuine smile.

Unimaginable even in the most talented writer's imagination, the metamorphosis was quick, precise and dramatic.

"Jeff, it's amazing how your face was just transformed!" I blurted.

"Joe, you have no idea how happy I am to see Shelby. I always feel so good when she's around. Shelby is very special. I think God chose her to accept the pain she went through because He knew she could handle it and now look at what great things she is doing."

An impenetrable silence invaded the room. The moment was far too emotional for words—but not a tear or two.

By now it was evident that Jeff was failing rapidly. Shelby felt the slow, steady drain of his life force. When she departed his company, after several more licks, I noticed her tail was low and still. Yet despite her sadness, depleted spirit and exhaustion, and in spite of the fact that she went to The Hackensack University Medical Center primarily to see one man, she spent the following three hours visiting and consoling most of the patients on Jeff's floor, amazing both physicians and nurses. Comforting people seemed to recharge her energy.

I felt a warm stirring in my heart to think of the many ailing individuals whose lives were so deeply touched by Shelby's compassionate presence, individuals whose pain and anguish were rendered more bearable because of her nurturing soul. She was certainly unique. Her first hospital visit had exceeded all my hopes and desires. Never would I have anticipated this empowering scenario. Undeniably, administering to the sick and suffering is Shelby's vocation.

Just a few weeks later, when Jeff was at home, I received a call from Brenna.

"Joe, Jeff's not doing well at all. He's asking for Shelby."

"Tell him we're on our way."

"Thanks…that should make him feel better."

At the sound of her name, Shelby immediately understood we were going to see Jeff. She also interpreted my mood, picking up on the gravity of the situation. Quiet and reflective, we walked out to the car, neither speaking a word.

When Brenna opened the door, Shelby wagged a greeting, in keeping with her well-mannered upbringing, and then made a mad dash for the sofa. It was empty. When she turned toward Brenna, I could see she was distressed.

"Shelby, Jeff is upstairs," Brenna said, clearing up the mystery and the anxiety. "Come with me—I'll take you to him. Jeff's waiting fo…"

Before Brenna finished the sentence, Shelby was on her way up the stairs. I followed, taking the steps two at a time, arriving just in time to see her crawl into bed beside Jeff. Maneuvering her by-now rather robust body, she inched her way up, careful not to cause unwarranted distress, placing her face next to his. I prayed I would not burst into tears in front of such a touching scenario.

Greatly weakened, Jeff reached out, settling his arm across her

Shelby provides comfort.

neck. I saw her tail wag, even if with difficulty, since she was lying on her side, occupying Brenna's spot. It was an absolutely amazing moment—man and dog were listening and understanding needs, relating, supporting, consoling and communicating like two soulmates in a deeply loving and committed relationship.

For a brief second I questioned if I would have believed my pup would have been able to assist a man on the final lap of his earthly journey—be his comfort and his solace, give him strength and joy, accompany him, hand in paw, over the thorny paths of his terrible illness, had I not witnessed it with my own eyes.

Brenna's entry into the room interrupted my thoughts. We

exchanged glances, not only because words would have been totally useless, but any vocalizations would have merely produced sobs.

Jeff managed to stay alert most of the time. He did not, however, close his eyes once when in Shelby's company.

"Jeff," Brenna said, flouting the silence, "did Shelby make you happy today?"

"Did she ever bring me such happiness and joy," Jeff blurted, taking a deep breath before giving my pup a kiss. His eyes, fixed on hers, seemed immovable. Then he raised his gaze to mine. "Well, Joe, you did, too—you brought me joy and happiness. You and Shelby are an awesome pair. Only God could have put you two together."

"Jeff, fear not—I will play second fiddle to Shelby anytime." His face brightened and his lips parted in a wide smile.

"Joe, Shelby's extraordinary. She's a dog with a human heart and soul. And I'm blessed to have her in my life." Even the self-control of a saint could not have kept me dry-eyed.

We shared a nice laugh and then it was time for me to take leave.

"Okay, Shelby," I said, as always, to signal we were leaving. No response.

"Shelby, we should let Jeff rest now. Come on, it's time to go home," I repeated. No response. Always meticulously submissive to my requests, my pup displayed an unexpected, willful disobedience.

"She doesn't seem to want to leave," Brenna said, chuckling. Tension was mounting. I was becoming restless, shuffling from one foot to another. *Why didn't Shelby obey?*

"Don't be upset with her," Jeff pleaded, anticipating my thoughts. "She knows. Shelby, I love you," Jeff crooned. "You have given me so much. You made my life joyful, even in suffering. Thank you...thank you. You are my angel."

Shelby nestled closer to Jeff, probably uncomfortably close. Her head and part of her chest were now firmly planted on Jeff.

I feared he would suffocate under the weight. Unhesitatingly, I stepped forward to intervene. Catching my move, Jeff held out his hand, motioning me to stop. I obliged as Shelby tenderly licked the face of her loving friend for the last time.

A soft whine was her 'goodbye, Jeff,' as, reluctantly but graciously, she climbed off the bed and headed for the stairs, too heartbroken even to gaze in my direction, as was her custom.

Shortly thereafter, Jeff was admitted to Hospice of New Jersey at St. Joseph's Wayne Hospital. I visited that same afternoon, intending to return in the evening. However, after dinner, a mutual friend phoned.

"Joe," she said in tears, "Jeff just passed away. It was peaceful and serene and he was assisted by an absolutely wonderful hospice staff." It was May 10, 2010.

"Please tell Brenna I'm so sorry. I have lost a truly great friend."

Shelby stood motionless beside my right leg. Suddenly she slid down on all fours, dropping her head on her front paws. Moist, glowing eyes and a dead-weight tail told me she was accepting of the Lord's will, but nonetheless devastated.

"Geralynn and I will be over in about a half hour."

"Thanks, Joe. Brenna will appreciate it."

In silence and mourning, we drove to the Rizzuto house. Midway, the phone rang.

"Joe, Brenna would like you to bring Shelby."

"Sure, I'd love to."

I made an abrupt, screeching U-turn and headed home to get Shelby. My compassionate, loving therapy dog had stepped into the new role of bereavement pup. I knew she would be thrilled, my special angel of mercy—anything for Jeff.

Sweet Shelb of Mine

"I am in favor of animal rights as well as human rights. That is the way of the whole human being."
—Abraham Lincoln

The weeks following Jeff's passing were difficult and anguishing for Brenna. Losing a beloved spouse can have devastating effects on the course of life, and with the addition of two children tender in age to comfort and succor, it becomes excruciatingly debilitating, often challenging faith and the ability to wean away from the gloomy darkness of despair.

Most grieving individuals seek therapists, support groups, clergy and close friends to assist them through the seemingly inconsolable moments following the death of a loved one. Brenna, nevertheless, chose Shelby, in her role as bereavement dog, as an adjunct to the conventional means of dealing with grief.

Of course, my pup was more than willing—and, I might add, competent—to handle the new position. Therefore, whenever Brenna phoned, I obliged. Jake and Alex, in particular, profited from Shelby's understanding, generous heart and ability to put smiles on the most devastated and grim faces.

Soft and gentle in her manner, loving and nurturing by nature and impassioned to focus on others instead of herself, she brought encouragement while teaching not only acceptance of the inevitable but the value of continuity in the forward movement of life.

"Joe," Brenna said after one of our visits, "thanks to Shelby's love and devotion during Jeff's trying illness, and thanks to John Flaherty's wonderful visit two days before his death, I think my husband's passing was serene. I think he went feeling loved and cherished. This gives me peaceful closure."

"It was too bad we miscalculated the time factor in getting tickets for the Yankee game. But I thought I'd make up for it by having a former Big League pitcher and sports announcer signing baseballs, t-shirts and hats for the boys at his bedside. It was an ultimate thrill. Plus it was great to hear Flaherty ask about Phil Rizzuto and Jeff proudly talk about his uncle's illustrious Yankee career. It brought back fond memories."

"It was a thrill, Joe—he was such a die-hard Yankee fan. But we're forgetting someone here—both Jeff and I had only words of praise and gratitude for you."

"Jeff was a great guy, Brenna—a loving husband, father and friend."

"Thanks—it's true. I have been blessed. But your darling Shelby—she's truly something extraordinary. Honestly, I don't know if I could have ever imagined a dog would be capable of such unconditional love, compassion and understanding. Kind of forces us to hang our heads in shame, don't you think?"

"Yes—for sure, it makes you reflect."

⌒⁓

Shelby continues her mission as an angel of mercy, serving those in need both as a therapy and bereavement dog, bringing joy and serenity to all who are blessed to enjoy her presence. Warm, loving and gentle despite the rash stereotyping of pit bulls as aggressive

Me and my girl, Shelby.

and often human-hostile animals, she quashes all these ignorance-based, preconceived ideas. In her own unique way, she is a poster dog for the anti-discrimination movement.

Reaching out to man, woman and child, regardless of race, religion, social status, political adherence and age, Shelby understands the need to love all God's creatures. Extending her *arms,* she offers solidarity and friendship, asking nothing in return. Every

Princess Shelby dons a crown.

tap of her paw, every warm nose nuzzle, every sweet, clean lick says, '*I love you, I care, I'm here for you, you're not alone. I understand your sadness. We can do this together—I'm your friend!*' And Shelby knows full well the agony of loneliness and abandonment, as well as the excruciating pain of physical abuse and humiliation. However, she has used her early destiny, a journey of suffering, for empowerment and for learning acceptance, tolerance and the joys of helping others overcome their own demons.

Always fascinated with the lyrics of Neil Diamond's "Sweet Caroline," I tweaked some of the words to portray my pup. Whenever I hear:

"Was in the spring and spring became the summer...
who would believe you would come along?
Hands touching hands...reaching out, touching me...
When I hurt, hurting runs off my shoulder from touching
    you...
how can I hurt when I'm with you?"

I sing:

"Sweet Shelb of mine...
paws touching hands...
eyes meeting eyes...
hearts greeting hearts...
nose nudging hand...
pain dissolving pain...
a life saving a life...
how can I hurt when I'm with you?
Oh, sweet Shelb of mine..."

In a sense, it is our special song.

Walking into my life and heart, joining my family, Shelby has inspired my professional juices. My new journey includes a series of exciting entrepreneurial ventures. I have branched out into motivational speaking and life coaching (www.proclaiming-treasures.com), relationship and obedience training for dogs (www.treasuretails.com) and my latest endeavor, pet loss counselor. All are targeted to improve, if not revolutionize, the quality of life both for humans and animals.

There is no cap on what my pup is willing and able to do for others. She moves forward, expanding her special mission on earth. Currently she is in the throes of spreading her angel wings to include serving children.

Geralynn has been in discussion with the Lincoln School in Nutley, New Jersey, for an autumn commitment on Shelby's part. Moreover, several funeral homes have expressed interest in her bereavement therapy, marveling at her unique ability to offer solace during funeral arrangements and further, according to the needs and desires of the individuals involved.

Shelby has no limits. She will serve all who call her, willingly and lovingly. Hers is a selfless assignment of unrestricted giving. This is who my pit bull pup is.

Although Shelby's story has been written, much remains to be lived—therefore, still to be written.

"It is truly amazing to see the transformation of Shelby. She has gone from a frightened pup to a happy, carefree one. It is heartwarming to see the way she follows Joe around the house. She has certainly found her forever home with us and has made a positive impact on all of our lives and the lives of everyone who met and will meet her."

—Geralynn Dwyer

"Yes, I saved Shelby. Yes, I trained her. But more importantly she saved me. She trained me. She instructed me on matters of faith. She inspired me and taught me the truth about life. And best of all she takes me with her on her journey to assist the needy and suffering. Shelby brings God's love to everyone she touches. If I could be half as successful in my ministry of service to all of God's creation, I'd consider myself a truly gratified man."

—Joe Dwyer

"If you would like to see me, just go to YouTube and type in my name. If you would like to keep updated on my adventures or write me, please go to my Facebook page. Thanks."

—Shelby Dwyer

www.shelbysgrace.com
shelby@shelbysgrace.com